# Working Class Audio Journal Volume I

Matt Boudreau



NextPoint Training, Inc.

ROWMAN & LITTLEFIELD
*Lanham • Boulder • New York • London*

Published by Rowman & Littlefield
An imprint of The Rowman & Littlefield Publishing Group, Inc.
4501 Forbes Boulevard, Suite 200, Lanham, Maryland 20706
www.rowman.com

6 Tinworth Street, London SE11 5AL, United Kingdom



Book design and composition by NextPoint Training, Inc.

Library of Congress Cataloging-in-Publication Data is available upon request.

ISBN 978-1-5400-4687-1

∞™ The paper used in this publication meets the minimum requirements of American National Standard for Information Sciences—Permanence of Paper for Printed Library Materials, ANSI/NISO Z39.48-1992.

Printed in the United States of America

# Working Class Audio Journal
# Volume 1

# Contents

# Acknowledgments

I believe things like the WCA Journal and WCA Podcast happen because of the direct and indirect influence and support of many people over the years. Interactions, conversations, ideas, and experiences with people led to decisions that ultimately formed the basis of these works. Seriously... I would have never come up with the Journal and Podcast had it not been for the life experiences I have had with other humans mentioned and not mentioned.

So here is a list of those I can assure you played a part in what you are reading.

**Family:** My wife Brenda and children Miles and Emerson as well as my brothers Mark and Steve, sisters Julie and Renee, and Mom and Dad. Family rules.

**Friends and colleagues in this volume:** Andrew Scheps, Kim Rosen, Mark Kilborn, and Langston Masingale.

**Friends and colleagues who helped in the creation of this book:** Eric Kuehnl, Frank D. Cook, and Mark Garvey.

**Friends and colleagues who have been on the podcast as of this writing:** All the guests that I've had the pleasure to interview on the podcast (see Appendix for a complete list).

**Sponsors of the WCA Podcast:**
Jules Standen and the crew at Gearslutz, Amanda Whiting Gerstle from Universal Audio, Gary Boss and Britney Groom from Audio-Technica, Daniel Holter and the crew at The License Lab, Simon Cote from Audio Plus Services, Brian Loudenslager from Lauten Audio, Jimmy Hua and Zach

McDermott from AEA Ribbon Mics, Matt McGlynn from Roswell Pro Audio, Colin McDowell of McDSP

A special thanks to all of you who have listened and got something out of the WCA podcast. I hope the WCA Journal brings you useful insight as well.

Did I forget someone? I bet I did. Regardless… I am grateful to them.

*Introduction*

# About Working Class Audio

Working Class Audio started as a concept in my head. It was a term that seemed appropriate for a new way of approaching my audio business after having stepped away, due to my own failures as an owner, from a studio I was running.

The studio (located in San Francisco) was a dream for me. It had the pedigree of having once been owned by Bill Putnam. He had redesigned the live room, and from that point on it was known as a "Putnam Room." It lived its life under many owners and names, including Mercury Recording (Mercury Records), Coast Recorders, Toast, and finally Broken Radio. Broken Radio in retrospect was a horrible name for a studio, but I thought I was being clever.

I made a series of missteps in my management of the studio. I overspent on gear and unnecessary construction, redesigning the control room. I failed to market the studio effectively. To top it off, I opened for business in June of 2007, just at the beginning of an economic crisis in the U.S. With all of these factors at play I became defensive about my dream and was in stone-cold denial of the severity of the situation.

I had basically jumped into the deep end and was unable to leave the pool. I had to stay in and keep my head above water. I took almost any work that came in the door. The positive side was that I really upped my recording game. The negative side was that my financial decisions were placing a strain on my family, and my relationship with my wife and the bank. Checks were bouncing, debt piled up, credit cards were maxed out, tears were shed, yet I marched forward with the determination of a racehorse complete with blinders on. Our second child was born in mid-2008, and the stress level went up another notch. There was business coming in, and money, but it was barely enough to cover the studio's expenses.

In 2011 the pressure was too much, and my wife pleaded with me not to renew the lease. I approached my building partner, Michael Romanowski, who had been running a successful mastering business in his half of the building, to ask for help. I explained the situation to Michael, and even though there was still time left on the lease he agreed to my getting off of the lease and took full responsibility for the rent and getting someone to take my place. The two of us were (and still are) like brothers and would fight and argue like brothers since joining forces in 2007. By 2011, I think we both were relieved to end the arrangement. After I signed off the lease, I was so anxious to go that I felt like I had given notice at a job and couldn't wait to leave the building. January 1, 2012, I woke up relieved not to be a studio owner. I was free; it was time to get out of the pool. The sadness about the situation I had put myself into had passed long before that point. I took all of my gear to my house and walked away with my tail between my legs. After years of working in audio, owning studios, and then getting my ass kicked by my own foot I asked myself, "Now what?"

I had to change my thinking and approach to my family, my audio work, my business, and money. I started listening to Dave Ramsey and slowly paying off debt. I set up a mixing setup at home, sold off gear I wasn't using, and played drums occasionally in cover bands to help bring in more money. It was during this time I started to call my way of working and thinking "Working Class Audio." I wanted to blog about this idea so I created workingclassaudio.com to do that. I also had questions for others like me. I wanted to know how they made it work, what journey they took, their approach to money and business, and the mistakes they made. That's when the Working Class Audio podcast was born.

Four years after starting the podcast I have interviewed over 200 audio professionals. As you would expect I have learned a great deal about those original topics I wanted to master. I'm also happy to report I am now out of debt, have a strong audio business of recording, mixing, and mastering, and my family life is solid. That said, the journey continues, albeit with a new perspective and approach all gained from trial and error.

The interviews in this book are taken from podcast episodes. You'll notice we don't get into technique or gear discussions unless it pertains to a story or idea. The whole concept is to discuss the journey, business, approach to money, survival, and work/life balance as those things pertain to an audio career. I hope the interviews in this book will give you some perspective and a few new ideas that help you navigate your own career. Just remember, making mistakes and failing is part of the journey. It's what you do with the experience learned from those failures and mistakes that counts.

Enjoy,

Matt Boudreau

## The Working Class Audio Journal Series

The **Working Class Audio Journal Series** represents a collaboration between NextPoint Training and Matt Boudreau that seeks to capture the essence of Matt's critically acclaimed *Working Class Audio* podcast in an easy-to-digest written form. Each volume features interviews with industry professionals that Matt has interviewed over the years.

These interviews explore the decisions and tradeoffs involved in pursuing a successful audio career, from business dealings and finances, to survival techniques in the studio and on the road, to finding an appropriate balance between work and personal life. Through the words of accomplished and respected individuals who have been there, you'll gain new perspective and ideas to help you navigate your own career.

## Volume I Interviews

This volume of the Working Class Audio Journal brings you interviews with four diverse professionals in the audio field:

- Engineer, producer, and label owner **Andrew Scheps** (Black Sabbath, Jay Z, Beyonce, Metallica)
- Mastering engineer **Kim Rosen** (Bonnie Raitt, Aimee Mann, Steve Earle, Kris Kristofferson)
- Audio entrepreneur **Langston Masingale** (owner of Handsome Audio and inventor of the Zulu passive analog tape simulator)
- Game sound designer **Mark Kilborn** (Forza Motorsport, Tony Hawk, Call of Duty, Black Ops)

# Andrew Scheps

## Backstory and Introduction

I originally met Andrew Scheps at Fantasy Studios in Berkeley, California, where he was giving one of his "Lost in Translation" presentations about lossy vs. lossless formats. After the presentation I joined Andrew and some mutual friends at the Missouri Lounge down the street for beers.

While we drank and talked shop, I quickly realized Andrew was not only one of the nicest people I had ever met but incredibly smart as well. He understood the bigger picture of record making as well as the minutiae that go along with it. It was also at that time I learned he worked with producer Rick Rubin, mixed Jay Z's *99 Problems*, and worked with many other high-level artists. It was exciting to be sitting there drinking beers with someone who had operated at what I considered to be the highest levels of the music industry, and the fact that he was so down to earth, warm, and friendly was refreshing. Based on his demeanor and how he treated others, this was someone I felt I could call a friend.

I stayed in loose touch with Andrew over time. We ran into each other at the PotLuck Audio Conference held in Tucson by my dear friend Craig Schumacher. We discussed his recent appearance at Mix with the Masters and our mutual admiration of Tchad Blake. Andrew told me that, like Tchad, he too was now mixing in the box. This revelation floored me because I was doing it as well, and to hear that someone with Andrew's credentials was doing it really gave me confidence in my decision.

Since then Andrew has grown into a household name in the world of recording. He's worked with everyone from Black Sabbath, Beyoncé, and Green Day to Jay Z and Metallica. In addition to being a great guy, Andrew is also a great educator, and I still watch his videos to steal his ideas on mixing.

Andrew graciously agreed to let me interview him in January of 2015 for the Working Class Audio podcast, and since then his has become the number-one downloaded episode from the series. While much has changed in Andrew's world since that interview, his words of wisdom still resonate to this day with many people. Enjoy.

-Matt

# Interview with Andrew Scheps

## Early Experience

Matt: I've known for a while, of course, that you mixed *99 Problems*, and to this day I think very highly of that mix. It's so powerful.

Andrew: Thanks, man.

Matt: You've been doing this for how many years?

Andrew: Well, I got out of college in '88 and started working for Synclavier, so I've been trying to make records full-time since '91 and did a little bit of touring early on because that's the work I got. So yes, basically since '91, I guess.

Matt: Did you go to University of Miami?

Andrew: Yes.

Matt: And then you worked for Synclavier, and you were a field rep that would go and make sure that the thing worked.

Andrew: Yeah, the field service tech. I went when it was broken, when I got a phone call.

Matt: You're the guy that gets all the wrath and all the glory at the same time.

Andrew: Yeah exactly. Every time you left they'd say, "Oh it was great to see you. I hope to never see you again."

Matt: At that point you got this early exposure to record making on a higher level because those who could afford a Synclavier were probably not making small–time records.

Andrew: Exactly. Those things were $100,000 to get in the door. By the end, when they had disk recording, you could probably spend half a million if you really wanted to.

Matt: Wow, that's a chunk of dough. When was the moment at which you started to make what I would classify as big–boy/big–girl records?

Andrew: That was more when I moved back into the engineering chair, which is where I'd always thought I was going to be. But pretty early on I was working on bigger projects because of things like the Synclavier, and then from there just being able to do a lot of keyboard programming and stuff like that. Then I was one of the very early Pro Tools guys. I would show up with my own rack of four DA-88s [tape-based digital multitrack recorders], do transfers, bring them back to my place, transfer it into Pro Tools, do a bunch of stuff, bring it back on DA-88s and transfer it back in sync onto your two-inch analog.

So, I wasn't necessarily always engineering or mixing or producing, but I was in on bigger sessions kind of from the very beginning, just because I had weird specific technical things that I was good at. You know, for a long time you would have an engineer and you would have an editor. Now very few projects can afford to have two people do that. I think what happened was, there were a lot of engineers who had a really hard time learning Pro Tools, whereas I was hot shit on Pro Tools and already could engineer, though no one was bothering to hire me for that.

I was just lucky, you know? I found ways to get myself in the room because of the more esoteric or technical side of things. But I always thought I was an engineer. It never occurred to me that I wasn't.... So, that transition was pretty natural. It was as the industry shifted, I was already right there.

Matt: Were you a staff engineer at a studio or a freelancer?

Andrew: I was always freelance, which I don't know that that's a good thing or a bad thing. I know Joe Barresi and some other friends of mine work at Sound City and got to work on a bunch of really cool records and learn a lot from other engineers and producers. And I never had that during that time. And that's what I thought I was going to do when I got out of school, but there was a job opening at New England Digital working on Synclavier, and I just took the gig.

It was money; it seemed interesting. I've always been a bit of a geek. I'm fascinated by the technology, so that's just where I went instead of working at the studio. And then from there, I didn't want to start back over again as a runner, but I wasn't really qualified to be an assistant. And I could also get in on sessions a little bit above the sort of assistant level. It's a parallel thing, it's not necessarily one is above another, but if I could get in there as an editor or a programmer or something like that and then end up doing some engineering along the way, it didn't make sense for me to take a gig as an assistant.

I just made sure that I learned as much as I could from every session I worked on as if I were the assistant, but I was actually getting paid to do some editing. And I would hang around, too. When I would have to take Pro Tools stuff away to work on it, I would stick around as long as I could. I was doing some editing on a Stones record that Don Was was producing. I didn't need to be there, but the band started showing up, and Ed Cherney showed up and they were going to start tracking and I just made myself very, very small and sat in front of the control room for like three hours. And then thought, "OK, I guess I'd better go get to work." So I got to be in a lot of situations where I didn't necessarily have any business being there, but that worked out.

## Studio Etiquette

Matt: Let's talk about something you said there: you became very small. That speaks to the control room or the studio etiquette. I talked to Craig Schumacher the other day, and he was just railing on an individual he encountered and said, "If this is the state of the student body coming out of these schools, we're in big trouble." Talk to me about what you find important in studio etiquette and in terms of the different people on the totem pole, if you will.

Andrew: There's a lot to say about that. The first thing is, I did a little interview for *Sound on Sound* and I sort of crystallized it into this: Just don't be a dick. That's the main piece of advice for anybody working in any field but basically, just don't be a dick.

But in terms of the hierarchy of things, what happens is, you're young and you're really technically savvy, and you know how to run the gear. That could be you know how to run a tape machine, you know how to use the console, you know how to

*"You've got to realize that the technical skills are something that should be a given, like you'd better be awesome on all that equipment. And the reason that other guy is in the room is because he's so good he doesn't need to be awesome on all that equipment."*

use Pro Tools, you know how to program Ableton—doesn't matter what it is. And you're working for an engineer who is older and more of a Luddite and maybe doesn't know how to do these things, and you immediately assume that you could do that guy's job.

It makes you arrogant and it makes you speak when maybe you shouldn't. You've got to realize that the technical skills are something that should be a given, like you'd better be awesome on all that equipment. And the reason that other guy is in the room is because he's so good he doesn't need to be awesome on all that equipment. It's understanding that, and it's tough. It's just part of being young, too.

I remember coming home from college and thinking I knew everything. I remember conversations with my parents, I'm still embarrassed about what a dick I was. We all go through it, but it's very, very important to learn how to read a room, to learn how to read how people are going to react to things, but to know your place and to know who you should say stuff to. I think there are many fewer kind of formal sessions in large studios with a producer and engineer and an assistant. But whenever you're in a situation like that, if you're the assistant and you think you've got an amazing idea, you don't tell the band. You tell the engineer and if the engineer thinks it's awesome, he will tell the producer, because he shouldn't tell the band.

And if the engineer takes credit for it, well, then he's being kind of a dick, but that's the role he's in and you've got to just learn to live within that system because otherwise, you're just going to get fired. You can't take over a session unless you're asked to or unless there's a real reason you have to.

Matt: So there is a chain of command, really.

Andrew: Yeah, and there has to be. There has to be because look, it's not an exact science. There's no right answer. If you notice something that's wrong, then it's your duty to point it out, but you have to point it out to whoever is next up the chain because otherwise, it can be seen as showing them up. It's such a weird, psychological, interpersonal experience in the studio that that's just the quickest way to get yourself out the door, and there's no need for it.

## Working with Rick Rubin

Matt: Switching gears a little bit, at what point did you start to do work with Rick Rubin?

Andrew: The first record I worked on for him was Saul Williams' *Amethyst Rock Star*. And then at the same time, there was a remix album of Wu-Tang songs that he was working on called *Loud Rocks*. There were two remixes he was producing; one, Rage Against the Machine, did a remix. Basically Tom Morello did that remix.

I don't remember if any of the rest of the band played on it. It may have just been Tom, and then Chad Smith played drums on that. And then I recorded some vocals for one that System of a Down did. That was somewhere around 2000, I would say.

Matt: OK, and was that a specific conversation? Did he approach you and say, "Hey, I really like what you do," or…?

Andrew: No, no, no. I was certainly beneath his notice in that way. I was brought in to do editing and keyboard stuff. The reason I got the call to work on the Saul Williams project is, they had been doing a lot of writing and tracking using MPC60 and a lot of stuff of that era. They were just printing stereo dumps of whatever was going on to do overdubs, and then they were mixing and wanted to split stuff out, and all of a sudden stuff wasn't syncing up anymore.

So he said, "Well OK, who can make this work?" And someone else who was working for him said, "Andrew can do that. He's a total geek. He'll make that work." That's why I got in there. I'd been called a couple of times before that to do some editing, and schedule–wise it didn't work out. But once you get in the room, if you are good and can do stuff.... I was there to basically do some programming, to make an MPC60 lock up to an analog tape machine. And then I ended up tracking Chad Smith playing drums on something the next day. So once you're there, you step up and do whatever comes up and then that's how you stay there.

Matt: It's good to be a problem solver, isn't it?

Andrew: Yeah, yeah because man, the last thing you need is more problems. But don't create problems, and if you can solve them, that's awesome. Especially if you can do it in a way that's transparent and just lets people work.

Matt: And it gives people a chance to become familiar with you, become comfortable with you, to invite you back into the room, I would assume.

Andrew: Yeah, yeah.

## Family

Matt: Talk to me a bit about your family. You have two kids, right?

Andrew: Yup.

Matt: And they're older now.

Andrew: They're older now, yeah. They're 23 and 19.

Matt: Talk to me about those early years, what you went through as far as family sacrifice. Did you miss birthdays? Did you miss Halloweens? You were obviously an up–and–coming guy and trying to become more of a household name, but you also had the responsibility of your kids.

Andrew: Our son was born when I was really young. It was right at the beginning. I hadn't really established myself at all, so it was tough. The toughest thing was that I got some touring work because of the Synclavier. I was on tour with Michael Jackson and then with Stevie Wonder. And those are long tours that go out for a while, and this is pre-internet. There's no Skyping, there's no cell phones, there's no email. I would have to wait for a production phone to be set up in the production office to call my wife.

That was really tough, and it coincided with our son being pretty young. The good thing is, that touring experience made those times when I was in town and working crazy hours seem like nothing. The other thing is that my wife completely understands what I do. I know a lot of musicians whose girlfriends or wives don't really buy into the fact that this is what they do because they're not really successful at it yet, and it's soul-destroying in a way because you know that it's your passion, it's your life and you really can't do anything else. And if you don't have somebody who understands that, they just think you're screwing around and that you're out late because you're wasting time.

There are very few times where I would stay at a studio just to hang out. I would go home. I mean, I liked to go home. But there are times when it's important to go have a beer with these people, and you've got to make sure you've got somebody who gets it. So fortunately, after the first few years I managed to be in town most of the time.

And there was also this thing of telling my wife, "Look, when the kids are out of the house, you're coming with me." I think for twenty years she didn't really believe that was going to happen, but then as soon as our daughter went off to college, that was it. She now goes with me, so now the traveling isn't that big a deal.

Also, I've had a studio at home for probably 20 years. Now more and more of my work is being done here, so now I almost never leave the house. But obviously I was still going to studios a lot early on in my career. But whenever I could, I would work at home and that's a huge thing, too. You just have to balance it. When I hear engineers say almost proudly that they missed the birth of their child because they were in the studio, I don't buy that.

I mean, I love what I do. It is my life's work. It's my life's passion in terms of working on music, but man, there's no record that's more important than a birth. It's just not. I think as long as you've got your priorities straight, it doesn't mean you're always going to be able to adhere to those priorities. But as long as you actually have them in that order, everything is cool.

It's when you don't. It's when you're staying in the studio to kind of avoid going home because it's fun to hang out and do a bunch of blow with the band.... You gotta go home.

Matt: Having your son early on, do you feel that that caused you to grow up a little quicker and prioritize maybe a little differently than someone who didn't have a kid at that moment?

Andrew: Yeah to a point, but I think it's probably just in my nature that I'm fiscally terrified. I'm always terrified that we're going to be living in a cardboard box because I'm not going to work enough. The more people you have depending on your income, the more that steers your decisions, but I would be terrified about money anyway. It's just the way I am. When people see pictures of the studio and they see all the gear, they're like, "You're terrified of money? No way, look at all the money you spent."

But if you look, very little of what's in here isn't going up in value. I don't just buy a bunch of new gear; I only buy old gear because it's going to hold its value, so when my career ends next week, I can sell it and live off it for a while. This is always in the back of my mind.

Matt: That's your retirement plan. We've talked about that.

Andrew: Yeah, absolutely. And it may end up having to be an earlier-than-retirement plan but, whatever it is, it is. And obviously I love my consoles. It's not that I only bought them as an investment, and I love that over the years I've used them a lot. But, it truly was an investment because I didn't trust myself to buy stock. I almost borrowed money to buy Apple. I came close to calling my parents to borrow money when they were at $13. It was right before they brought Steve Jobs back. I thought, "Man, they're not going to go under." I was so terrified that I couldn't bring myself to do it. When Vance [Powell] told me he bought it at $100, I was just like, "Aahh!" But these things happen. I'll live with it.

## Business Survival

Matt: I do want to talk about gear in a little bit because you're tempting me with talking about your consoles, but I'm going to hold off for a second. I want to talk a little bit about survival. When you're at the level that you're at, I think there's probably the perception, by other engineers out there that, "Oh, Andrew Scheps... I mean, (a) he must be rolling in it, and (b) he's going to have a never-ending career."

Andrew: Yeah, that's not true at all. I was introduced to somebody once, and the guy who was introducing me mentioned a couple of the records I'd worked on. And as he shook my hand, this guy said,

"Oh, you must be a very wealthy man." I'm like, "You have no fucking idea."

Matt: Give us the reality on the ground. You don't have to talk specific numbers, but give us the true reality.

Andrew: Well, the true reality is that except in a few specific cases, there are very few records that have big budgets anymore, and certainly in the genres that I choose to work in the most. If I really wanted to chase doing more pop records, I could probably find some bigger budgets, but I'm also up against people who've been doing that for years. I don't know that I can compete with Manny [Marroquin], Tony [Maserati], Serban [Ghenea], and those guys in that world. And I don't know that I really want to because it's not what I do.

So, budgets are tiny. They're a tenth of what they were five years ago. And that's OK. I can still pay my mortgage, but I do tons and tons of projects for very, very little money. And then every once in a while, there's something that's got a good amount of cash and that's great. There are also very, very few projects that I have points on, and of those, almost none of them have ever been worth a penny. So, there is this myth.... It's the same myth like bands make all their money touring.

Well, that's not true either. We could go through how they actually lose a bunch of money touring, but we only have so much time. But it's that perception that, "Oh man, that guy's got points. He's fabulously wealthy." Obviously it's like playing the lottery. Like if I had points on Adele, I would be rich. I would've gotten hundreds of thousands of dollars off of that, but I don't so I didn't.

I basically work for my fees, and I'm sure everybody you've talked to has said the same thing. The fees are absolutely not what they used to be. That's the reality. I'm always looking for work and always negotiating the best deal I can and I'm always cutting people deals.

Matt: You listened to my interview with Vance Powell. I don't know if you remember this portion of my talk with him, but, as far as how you got management and Vance's description of it, is it pretty much the same thing?

Andrew: I think one thing is that engineers and producers look at management the way bands look at getting signed. They think it's this Holy Grail and something will be solved about their career. I mean look, the typical thing that a manager takes is 15 percent, so your reasoning going into it needs to be that you feel that management will generate at least that much more work so that after commission, you still make the same amount of money.

You'd love it if it was even more money than that. The idea is that they manage your career, right? They'd help you make decisions. And as Vance pointed out, and it's one of the most important things, they have the conversations that you really shouldn't be having with the creative people. Let the money people talk to money people and then that way, even though you're the one telling them what to say, what you will accept and what you won't accept, you're not the one saying it to their face right before you try and track a vocal.

That's a huge part of it. Obviously me not having to collect my own money anymore, that's massive, but you could do that with a business manager instead, if you wanted to, for 5 percent or whatever they charge. For me, I love my manager. I think Frank McDonough is an awesome guy. He's got a great roster. The way I got hooked up with him was through another really good friend of mine, Joe Barresi, who Frank has managed for longer than he's managed me.

To be honest, the first time I talked to Frank he said, "I don't think you're ready." I'm like, "OK, cool," and the next time I talked to Frank, it was right in the middle of when we were making *Stadium Arcadium* with the Chili Peppers and I was about to start working on a Linkin Park record. He said, "Yeah man, let's do this. But you've already got those gigs lined up, so why don't we start it up after Linkin Park?"

Immediately I knew that this guy is not in it just for the money. If he were, he's in the wrong business. But there are a lot of them who are just super greedy. There are a lot of people who hate it when the producers on their roster hire an engineer who isn't on their roster because that's part of the budget they're no longer getting 15 percent on, and that's ridiculous. You need to make the best record you can make so you need the right people for it, period. We're making art. We're not like, "Oh, going to get some quotes on putting up a shed in my garden."

Frank is not like that. For me, his style of management is something that fits in with my personality. I feel as if some people want their manager to be a total dick so they don't have to be, but to me, my manager is me. He's representing me. He's my avatar in these meetings. That's a big part of it.

Now, there has definitely been work that has come through Frank, but it's because he's got a roster and people will call him up and say, "Hey man, I got this project. Who do you think would be good for it?" That's how that happens. It's not that he's out pounding the pavement getting me work, it's just that he has relationships with people who have work. That's how that happens.

And look, there are times when I'm super frustrated. Like last year, I had a three-month period where I did not work, basically. I don't think I had a single paying gig for eight weeks. And within the three months, I worked on maybe two things that paid money. So, it can get really bad and you'll start to blame management, but then you talk to everybody else and they're slow too and then something picks up. It goes in waves and it's definitely not the silver bullet that's going to cure all your ills. But when you're at a point where you're spending more time chasing up money and doing deals than working on music, then you're probably ready to have a manager, I would say.

Matt: In terms of demystifying, would you say to bands that may be listening to this, you're available.

Andrew: Yeah, of course.

Matt: You're approachable.

Andrew: Absolutely, and look, you almost don't need to even say that because I've stopped looking at Facebook messages. I saw yours purely by accident, because I get about 30 a day from bands. I don't even want to open it because I feel bad if it says, "seen at whatever time" and I don't respond, but I can't. I can't physically listen to every single person who sends me stuff.

One thing that's good about that is if you send it to my manager, he actually will compile things and send them to me and I have a much better chance of seeing it. But yes, I'm absolutely available. I'm always looking for great stuff to do and, you know, it's not $10,000 to mix, believe me. I don't know who the hell gets $10,000, but someone does I'm sure.

I don't want to say I'm cheap, but I'm very flexible. I'm mixing records right now for very little money but because I either have a relationship with the people or I love the music. There are a million reasons why I would do a project, and it's certainly not about the money most of the time.

Matt: That's good to hear and I think a lot of bands hearing this would love to have you work on their stuff.

Andrew: Yet at the same time, please don't be offended if I don't get back to you. I just can't keep up with it now. I really can't.

Matt: And they can go to your manager's website.

Andrew: Yeah, it's mcdman.com. There's a contact link there and you can find me. And I almost feel like I need to post on Facebook to say this so that people know not to get upset if I don't get back to them but, Facebook messages is not the way to get ahold of me.

Matt: Yeah, I think in the past I've emailed with you.

Andrew: Yeah, it seems as though Facebook messaging is getting pretty ubiquitous. When I started my label, which I'm sure we're going to talk about at some point, years ago, I started accepting every single friend request. I made like 4,800 friends and I know maybe 12 of them. But I get messages constantly so I just have decided that that's not a place I'm going to actually look for information.

## Tonequake and Diversification

Matt: Let's talk about the label. Tonequake?

Andrew: Tonequake.

Matt: I was going to ask you about diversifying as a survival strategy, and I don't know if having a label counts.

Andrew: The joke is: You know how to make $10 million in the music industry, right? Start with $20 million. As far as diversifying to survive, I would say that starting a label is a really bad idea. As far as diversifying to understand what is actually going on in the world, I think it's pretty smart. There's so much about getting a record out into the world and getting it noticed.

One of the reasons I stopped reading the Facebook messages is I get a million of them that say, "Hey, I'm really talented and I just need to get my stuff mixed by you and then it's all going to explode." And man, that's not the case. One of the reasons I started my label is because there's so many amazing records I made from major labels that they screwed up the release or that they didn't screw up the release, but they just didn't catch on for whatever reason.

That side of the music industry is so brutally hard, unfathomable, impossible to control, and expensive that I think it's good to dabble in it for a minute and get an appreciation for the people who are actually really good at it. That's a big deal. And just to the topic of diversification first before we go into anything else you want to talk about with the label, I think it's really important.

I've always been diverse: I engineered, and did Pro Tools editing, and did keyboard programming and whatever. Now at this point, I have my label which loses money, but I suppose has the potential to make money. But I did the plug-in with Waves, which I'm actually really proud of and I think is awesome. It doesn't generate any money for me, but I do things like this. I do podcasts, I do interviews, I do articles. I don't know if any of that is ever going to turn into any money, but I feel like at this point after this long, I have some stuff that's important to me to say, and if I'm given a platform to say it I would be an idiot not to take advantage of it.

Matt: When I talk about diversification, for me at my level, diversification means in addition to this podcast, I actually edit a human resources podcast for a guy in Connecticut as side money two to three times a month. It's a little chunk of money and it definitely pays some bills. Have you ever gone down that road, not necessarily podcasting, but… have you ever done other stuff not related to music?

Andrew: Early on, I almost took a full-time job cutting sound effects, but I did it freelance for a while. I would show up and do ads, and I remember conference calls about the sizzle sound when we were doing an ad for the Play-Doh McDonald's set. That was a drive-through and you could press a hamburger out of brown Play-Doh. We had a conference call about which sound effect we were going to use for the sizzle when you press down the Play-Doh, so yeah, I've done all kinds of stuff.

And I think that it's great because first of all like you say, it's a chunk of change. It's also, you learn about stuff. Records is a tiny, tiny, tiny part of the audio world in terms of work. If you can get yourself a union gig taking care of audio at NFL Network and you happen to like football, that might be a much more fulfilling way to earn a living doing some audio. There's so

*"[Making] records is a tiny, tiny, tiny part of the audio world in terms of work. If you can get yourself a union gig taking care of audio at NFL Network and you happen to like football, that might be a much more fulfilling way to earn a living doing some audio."*

many things, like gaming audio, either from sound design or from music. There's more money there than in films now.

That sort of diversification I think is really important, and it's also important because you just learn stuff. You learn how to do things. You learn to appreciate it. Like cutting dialogue is difficult, cutting sound effects is as creative as writing songs. It's a real great insight into other people's creative process, which is always worthwhile.

If you're in a creative industry, trying to see how other people are creative is pretty important. But just from a work standpoint, yeah absolutely. At this point I'd like to pretty much just do records, but that doesn't mean that something wouldn't come up that seems interesting or I just need the work and I will do it.

Matt: Yeah. Well, let's delve into the label. Why did you want to do a label?

Andrew: Purely because I thought I could do it better. Like being the assistant thinking you can engineer better, I was making records and thought that I'd seen the labels drop the ball in how they put it out or when they put it out or decisions they made, or not putting it out at all. I just felt like, "OK, I'm going to have a label one day." You say this over beers for 10 years or 15 years, and then an opportunity came up with a particular record for this band Low Roar.

We just decided to do it ourselves and that started the label. And I didn't want the band to put it out. I wanted it to be a label. I had some specific ideas about the aesthetic of the label. Not musically, but just how it would be. I got talked out of a few of them, and I'm sort of glad I did. I wanted to be just sort of like a lemonade stand at the end of a driveway like, "Hey, I've got some music here."

But I quickly found out that basically, you would sell it to your mom and nobody else if you do that. You do have to do some promotion and you have to do some radio work depending on the type of music. So, I got sucked into the same world that all the other labels are in but trying to be very hands on and to question everything along the way, like, why does it have to come out on Tuesday?

That's been the thing that bugs me the most since I started the label. Just to be a pain in the ass, I didn't want it to come out on a Tuesday, and every record I put out has come out on the Tuesday. And it still bothers me, because there's no reason for it. But, that's what happens because that's the cycle. That's when people are used to it.

That's why I decided to start it, and I've picked up a few other acts along the way, which has been great. I've got some great music on there I think. But really the Low Roar project is the only one that's really kind of doing anything at the moment.

Matt: In that case, does the band... Do they pay you for the recording element of it, or are you doing it for free?

Andrew: The way the label works is, I license finished records from the band. Now, it turns out that I've worked on most of the records that I've put out. Not all, but I've worked on most of them. And, like in the case of the Low Roar records, the first record, basically Ryan—the main songwriter/singer—and I made the record with a couple other people playing stuff. This last record they're very much a band. It's a three-piece band. I still co-produced and added a bunch of instruments and mixed it, so I'm very creatively involved in those records.

Some of the other stuff I put out I've just mixed, but my deal for making the record is completely outside of the label. The label does not sign artists; it licenses masters, just because it's a cleaner way to deal with it. It's a straight up 50/50 split once we recoup and it's 70/30 in my favor until we recoup. But also, I don't recoup the way record labels recoup. Are you aware of the crazy economics of how you recoup if you're a band signed to a major label?

Matt: I was on Warner Brothers and a label called Imago many years ago, but I don't remember.

Andrew: I've talked to a lot of bands who've been signed forever who don't know how much they're actually getting screwed. Basically, if you sign as an artist to a major label, you get about 12 points. That's sort of a standard deal on the record sales. And then you've got X amount of money that you have spent to make the record and that's a recoupable expense. You don't make that amount of money selling records to recoup the expense. Your 12 percent of the record sales has to be that amount before it's recouped.

Which means they're selling eight times the record budget. So if you spent $100,000 making a record—which these days is unheard of, but let's say you spent $100,000—you would have to sell almost $800,000 worth of records before your 12 percent had recouped that $100,000. That's insane. That's just jiggery poker on a spreadsheet to me. That's crazy. So, when I say it's a 70/30 split, it's basically I get 70 cents of every dollar that comes in until I break even, and then we just split everything 50/50. But that's of 100 percent of the money. There's nothing coming off the top for anything. That's generally the deal I cut with the band. In fact, I think that is the deal on every single record I've put out.

And then in terms of what I spend, it just depends on the release. Like the Low Roar records, we've spent tons of money. We've done PR campaigns in Europe, in South America, in the States. I've done radio in the States. I've paid for tour support for them in the States and in Europe. I spent a ton of money on other releases. Oh, and I've also pressed vinyl and CDs on both Low Roar records. We're even selling the high–res version of the new Low Roar record. On other ones, I've only pressed CDs and done radio or done a little bit of promo. Then there are a couple that are only out digitally and if the artist wanted to do some promo, that's on them. So every release is different in terms of the scope.

Matt: Since the label is licensing the record, when it comes to your duties as producer–engineer, is the band paying for that or not?

Andrew: That deal is completely outside of the label deal. If I'm going to get paid to do it, they just pay me to do it. One example of that on my label is Twenty Two Hundred, this great rock band from Australia. They hired me to mix the record; I mixed the record. I got paid to mix the record; that was it. Then they came back a few months later and said, "Hey man, we've been thinking about it and we want you to put it out," at which point we decided who was going to pay to press the CDs and that was the money that needed to be recouped.

But the fact that they hired me to mix their record has nothing to do with the money that the label makes. It's purely based on sales of the record to recoup the costs of selling the record. That's it.

Matt: That keeps it clean.

Andrew: Keeps it super clean. So whatever the deal is for making the record has nothing to do with the label. In the case of some of them, there's no money at all and I love it and I'm very involved. In that case, that's a deal I would work out whether I had a label or not, where maybe I'd get a piece of the songs because that's the only way they can pay me or they'll owe me money if they get this or that or the other thing. You'd just be as creative and flexible as you can be so that if it does really well you'll get paid, but they're not trying to come up with money for something before they've actually made it.

Matt: Do you end up spending a lot of money on lawyers?

Andrew: No, very little actually. I spent money when I started the label to get a one–page contract drawn up and that's what I use with every single band.

Matt: Excellent.

Andrew: We're not talking about a lot of money here. If one of these explodes and we're talking about a lot of money, they're going to get upstream to some major label who can actually service them well. I don't have a staff of people. I would have to hire outside everything to service something if it explodes, so it's going to be out of my hands long before we're talking about anything that is difficult to take care of.

I just wanted to be completely upfront. I mean, I can't imagine how many pages it takes in a contract to explain to somebody that only 12 percent of the income from selling the record goes against the debt that they've incurred by letting the label pay to make the record. There's no way they spell that out in one sentence because the bands would call bullshit on it. They'd say, "Well in that case, give me 50 points. I understand you have overhead because you have offices and administration. You've got overhead that isn't directly tied to my record and it's got to get paid for, but not 88 percent."

So, the contracts are very, very simple. The typical reason I need to actually pay lawyers is because most of my artists are not in the US, and when they come to the US, they need visas. That costs me more money in legal fees than everything else I've done combined.

Matt: Oh my gosh! And what a hassle.

Andrew: Yeah, because if you want it any quicker than six months away, you have to pay the expedite fee, which is like 10 times the regular fee. It's insane.

Matt: Wow! Just hearing you say it makes me want to stay away from it.

Andrew: Yeah, you should.

Matt: I think I'd rather just stay making records.

Andrew: Yeah.

## Mixing in the Box

Matt: Let's talk a little bit about gear. I think the number one thing that has really been on my mind personally, and something that gave me fantastic vindication that also made me feel good about my decisions, was when I ran into you in Tucson this last time around and you said you're mixing in the box. I thought, "All right, Andrew's doing it. I sure as hell am going to be doing it, or continue to do it."

It's interesting because I've gone through various incarnations of high–end Pro Tools systems and spent thousands of dollars, as I'm sure you have, and many others have. And it used to be my perception that it was a taboo thing that, "Oh, you're mixing in the box. Well, that's not very pro. That doesn't sound good at all."

But to hear somebody like you, whose work I personally admire, say it, it really makes me feel better that I'm doing it. I would never compare my work to your work because we're just at different skill levels I think.

Andrew: No, no, no, no, no.

Matt: But back to the point, the point is, you're mixing in the box. People know that you have this studio full of gear. And they know you have a couple Neve boards. So, why did you do this?

Andrew: Well, our friend Vance Powell would have you believe it's because I have a particular client.

Matt: Oh that's right, he did say that.

Andrew: He did say that, but the reality is, I haven't actually worked for him in over a year. That's sort of old news. But obviously, there are the workflow differences. When you mix on a console, the mix is on the console. I've got 18 knobs and a fader, plus about eight switches, on every single module of the console and I've got a 64-input console, so you can do the math. That's how many settings need to be written down to document a mix. And a lot of the knobs on the Neve are not stepped. So, you're sort of drawing a picture of where that line is pointing. There are a lot of arguments about, "Well, just take a picture." Well, the knobs are more than an inch tall so the parallax makes it so that you have no idea what you're looking at unless you're directly over the knob.

Anyway, documenting the mix is very difficult, which means you can't work on a mix then take it off the console, and then put it back on the console and expect it to sound the same because it won't. It absolutely won't. And I've never had it sound better. It's always worse every single time.

So, that workflow means that you then have to change how you work with clients. You have to say, "I'm mixing one song at a time. You have to get back to me. It sits on the console till it's done." Then you start to be very, very aware of the amount of time it's going to take you to do a mix. Not the time it's going to take me personally to do the mix, but the time that mix will be on the console. And if you're working with someone in a different time zone, days get lost just waiting for mix notes.

That obviously can be very frustrating, and back when there was more money on a lot of projects, I would split my fee between studio time and a mix fee. They would just pay for the number of days that it took. So then I'm OK with it. I'm making less money the longer it takes, but I'm still making a bit more money than I would have in that period of time because they're paying by the day. People can't afford to do that anymore.

The other thing is, people don't understand the concept of, once I take that mix off the console it's done. They're like, "No." They still will call you two and a half weeks later and say, "We're going to need the high hat down a little bit," and, "I need a version like this." That's just the reality of the way people think about making records. It's been 25 years since anybody thought about making records that way, and over the last 25 years, just more and more and more and more flexibility and recallability are the norm.

That was my impetus to see about going back to mixing in the box because obviously, I started mixing in the box. I wasn't born with a Neve console. I've had these for the last seven years or something like that. And I learned on a console so that made sense to me. But then when I could only afford Pro Tools, there you go. Once they had hardware inserts, I figured out how to manually delay compensate and I started using that a little bit. Then once delay compensation came back in and was working, that was a huge deal.

At that time let's say, I don't know, 10 years ago, mixing in the box absolutely worked, but it didn't sound great. It really didn't. It sounded good, but it wasn't amazing. Mixing in the box now, I am convinced from having done shootouts with myself that it actually sounds better in a lot of cases than mixing on the console.

Now another thing... I'm jumping all over the place here, but it's such a massive topic that it's hard to keep one train of thought going.

Matt: You go man.

Andrew: I'm going to pull on to the siding that talks more about workflow and how you could maybe work the way I used to work on the console but still accommodate people who want to do recalls. I think Vance does that by printing stems of everything, and then he can tweak his mix from the stems. But, I don't work the same way Vance does. I've got lots and lots of shared parallel compression, which means I've got multiple instruments going into the same compressor. They don't all have external key inputs so I could print what's going to them and then use that as a key input.

It's impossible for me to print stems that add up to the mix. It cannot be done. So, I would have to print stems very early on in the mix and then just mix in the box anyway so what's the point of that? I would much rather be completely flexible.

I think there are two reasons why mixing in the box actually sounds better to me now. One is, stuff just sounds better. The Pro Tools mixer going to floating point really threw me for a while. I had to get used to it but now I love it. The headroom is great. You can change things much more easily down the chain with master faders and gain structure without having to undo things you've done because it's floating point. It retains all the overs that were there in the mixer and you can pull it down anyway. It's a lot of technical bullshit, who cares? But, that makes it easier. It also sounds better. And the plug-ins sound way better than they used to.

One of the reasons I'm liking the sound of what I'm doing in the box better in a lot of ways is also, to mix on a console, lets say I'm splitting out across 40 channels on my desk. No matter how many tracks it is, I'm coming out 40 outputs. That's 40 D/A's [digital-to-analog converters]. The D/A, if you know anything about building digital things, the D/A is by far the weakest link in any digital chain.

It's the most susceptible to clock, and then you've got the analog electronics on the backside of it so if things are loud, you're going to start crunching in the analog domain because it maybe can't handle the level or the transients. And you're also going through it so you have to like the sound of it. And then, you have to go back into Pro Tools, so you're going back through an A/D [analog-to-digital converter], which is not as problematic, but it is still a conversion.

If I'm mixing 100 percent in the box, the first time—assuming the mastering is done digitally—the first time since the microphone and the A/D on the way in that the thing is decoded is when you listen to the record. That's pretty cool and that gets rid of all of the possible weak points or little jittery crap that can happen going through D/A's during a mix process.

Not to mention the fact that I don't respect gain structure a whole lot. I'm slamming analog gear a lot louder than it's meant to and that makes things collapse in a good way. I love the way that sounds, and for all the years I've mixed in the console, that was what was great about it to me. But that's also why I was always having trouble with stereo image, keeping it wide, because you start getting crosstalk in places that normally you wouldn't.

Yeah, I'm just convinced that those are some of the reasons why I like it better. But I have literally done shootouts with myself mixing the same exact song on a console and then in the box. One right after another from scratch, and I've done it twice with two different things in two different studios. Both times the in-the-box mix won, and not in subtle ways. It destroyed it.

Then from there, I can start to enjoy all of the workflow awesomeness that there is with working in the box because I don't have to wait for approval. I send a mix and then I immediately start working on something else. I'm never only working on one thing at a time. As soon as I find myself losing focus, when I was mixing on the console, what do you do? You play Solitaire, you leave the room, you go have lunch and then you come back and that time has passed. Now I open up another song.

I will be mixing eight or 10 songs at a time and I cycle through them. And as soon as I don't know what I want to do next on a mix, open up something else, which also means if I'm mixing a record that's all tracked similarly, I can figure something out on song number six on the third day of mixing all eight, that I can then apply to all eight and see if it actually makes all eight of them better. Instead of discovering that on song six and trying to decide, "Man, is it worth recalling the first five?" which is something that used to happen a lot.

You really are struggling with something—with, let's say, the drums—and they were all tracked at the same place, and then you figure it out. And now like, "Man, do I go make the first five songs better or not?" Because then that's on you. Now, I can absolutely go do it and it won't necessarily waste a whole lot of time to try it because I'm just importing [those settings]. Plus there's all the stuff about having a template, which is not that big a deal because I used to leave tons of gear patched up ready to use, so I always sort of had a template. But it's more flexible and it's more gear. I don't have to run out of busses. I have as many busses as I want and I can just import things quickly.

So, all of the really obvious stuff that everybody loves about mixing in the box, I'm now getting that benefit. But I wouldn't do it if I didn't think it sounded better, and for me right now, the way I'm mixing it sounds better.

Matt: Yeah, I love it. It brings me satisfaction to hear you say that.

Andrew: And to back it up, it's not just me. I've had many more times when mastering, it's a flat transfer with zero changes—and from people who notoriously like to tinker. They say, "Look, I don't know what to do with this. This sounds awesome." The frequencies are right, the imaging's right, they're fine. All of that is working out at the moment. And who knows man, in six months I might hate the way it all sounds and do something different. But at the moment, that's what's going on.

Matt: You're saying in the box, so I'm assuming you're 100 percent in the box.

Andrew: 100 percent. My mix rig fits in a backpack.

Matt: You want to just give me a brief rundown of that? What are you using?

## Gear

Andrew: It's a MacBook Pro. When I'm home I've got a Thunderbolt Chassis with two HDX cards in it, which is great for track count. I don't necessarily need that, though. I originally had the two cards because I was driving 80 [channels of] I/O, which I don't need to do. I've only got one I/O on at the moment. And then when I'm traveling, I just don't bring the HDX cards. A lot of studios will have Thunderbolt Chassis now, so I can just plug in and use their cards. Or if I don't have that, then I just have the computer.

Then I also have an Octo card, a UAD Octo card, and an Apollo Twin. When I'm on the road, the Apollo Twin is also my little control room [for] headphones. And that's it. I've got a Frontier

Designs Alpha Track, which is a little one–fader controller. Yeah, that's it.

Matt: Wow! That's shocking. Are there any records recently done in the box by you that people might not know were done in the box? Can you name any of those?

Andrew: Well, this is going to make me sound like such a dick. "Just look at The Grammy nominations and you'll see them" [laughs]. There are three records that I did that are actually up for Grammys this year and they were all in the box. Beyoncé, Ziggy Marley, and Hozier. All 100 percent in the box. And the great thing is, what that means is I could work on them anywhere. I went to Europe last year for a little while and I did some of that mixing on the road.

It doesn't matter where I am. People don't need to know where I am. I mix when I mix, and it's the exact same rig no matter where I am, and it's awesome. It's freed me up in ways that are... it's life changing.

Matt: Does that mean you're mixing on headphones?

Andrew: Sometimes. And that scares me, but so far I haven't had any complaints. One of the flat transfers was mastered at Abbey Road and they love to do stuff. They've got amazing gear there and the guys there are really great. I sent the mix and I warned the A&R guy to let me know if there was any problem. He showed up half an hour after the start of mastering because they wanted to give the guy some time with it.

He walked in and the Abbey Road mastering engineer said, "Well, you paid for another hour so we could run it through some stuff but I've already done a flat transfer, and it's done. There's nothing to change." So, I've gotten lucky with it. Ten years ago there's no way I could've done a mix on headphones and have it sound like anything. It's just experience and whatever. It's my 10,000 hours that have gotten me to that point so I don't think there's any magic to it, but it is at that point.

I'd actually prefer to have speakers all the time, but that's not always possible. I would rather keep being able to work and do whatever it is that I'm doing in my life that has me away from a pair of speakers than to say I can't go to my mother–in–law's place in England, or I can't go to Iceland for Iceland Airwaves when Low Roar is playing a little string quartet in front of 1,500 people. I want to do those things, but I also, I can't not work because I'd be broke.

Matt: What headphones are you using?

Andrew: Man, it's so funny because it's the Sony MDR-7506. The super-bright headphones that everybody has in their studios because drummers can actually hear things over their drums. It's just the headphones that I happen to own because I bought five pairs for my studio. And it's not like I know them that well. I guess I do because I've owned a pair of Sony headphones for years. But when I'm at home I don't mix on them. It's not like I'm used to mixing on them.

The thing that's good about them is they're bright, so you can hear what's going on, whereas a lot of really good–sounding headphones are actually kind of dull. Everybody worries so much about the low end, but I think there are way more mistakes made in the high frequencies where stuff is harsh and building up and stepping on each other—cymbals stepping on guitars, stepping on vocals. If you don't clear out your upper mids and top end, that's going to be a much bigger problem than not clearing out your low end.

You can always shave off the low end and it'll just be kind of a bummer, but you can do it without destroying things. You can't sort out bad mid-range and top end, and it's really easy to hear on these headphones. And I think for the low end, you just get used to what the low end does to the frequencies above it—like I can tell what the bass and kick drum are doing by how the vocal sits in the track. Everything affects everything else so much that you don't really have to listen specifically for low end, I don't think.

Matt: When you are mixing on monitors, what's your two favorite monitors of choice?

Andrew: Tannoy SRM 10Bs, and if I had to pick two, I would pick one for the left and one for the right. Seriously, I don't use any other speakers.

Matt: OK, so you're not an NS10 guy?

Andrew: No. I have a pair because for years I had them, and I keep them around so if somebody comes to attend a mix there's a pair of speakers they know if they really want to check it. But that doesn't come up a whole lot. Usually what'll happen is, the band will come in, they'll hear my speakers, which feel kind of bright, they'll want to listen on the NS10s, and either by the end of that first day or by the second day, we never listen to them again.

Matt: Interesting. I want to shift gears for a little bit. I want to ask about mistakes. What are some critical mistakes that you've made that you've really learned from that you're open to talking about?

Andrew: Well, I didn't buy Apple at $13, that's number one.

Matt: That's number one.

## Making Mistakes

Andrew: I'm almost as terrified of making a mistake as I am of losing money, so I tend to be ridiculously over–prepared for things. I feel like I'm good at reading situations and sort of knowing what's coming next, so I'm generally pretty prepared for stuff. Very early on in my career, I did an internship in Music Annex up in the Bay Area. I was assisting on a session, and this is before I learned the hierarchy of the studio. I had an idea about a guitar part, and I voiced it, and fortunately the producer was awesome and kind of got me to shut up in a very subtle way during the session.

He said, "Hey man, let me take you out to dinner tonight," and I got the talk about how it all works and how it should work, which as soon as he said shut up, I didn't even need to talk anymore. But, he was very, very cool and explained it all. That's a simple mistake. In terms of whether I ever erased something or not, I'm sure I did back on tape. I'm sure I blew punches all the time. I don't know though.

I don't think I've made too many, I mean in terms of the kind of mistake that I would classify as a mistake; it would be like some sort of decision in my career where I didn't take a gig I should've, and I don't believe that that's really happened. It's not this sort of Zen, everything-happens-for-a-reason kind of thing, but I've been really lucky in my career. The only mistakes I've made are doing things because I thought somebody else wanted me to do it, or it would be perceived to be a good thing, and not really following my gut.

I had a manager before Frank, and it seemed like a mistake going in and it turned out it was a mistake and so I just stopped working with them. There are plenty of things like that where I'll have a gut feeling about something and either follow it or not and then I find out whether I'm right. I don't know. Maybe I don't want to dwell on the mistakes because they just make me feel bad. Give me an example. Maybe I'm thinking the wrong scope of mistakes.

Matt: No, no, no. I trust that you would know. There was one mistake I made early on. I made this singer, this woman, I made her cry in a session and really learned a deep lesson there about keeping my cool.

Andrew: I fortunately got to learn a lot of those lessons by watching other people fuck up.

Matt: Well, you must've been in the room quietly.

Andrew: I learned what not to do, even if it's just for you. You know like, "Oh, that's that guy's style, but I don't want to be like that." But definitely learning just how to be a good person in the studio. That's a huge part of working on records, is the personality, because people are trying to be creative, which means they're vulnerable and all the rest of it. Fortunately, I think I learned most of those lessons by watching other people screw up.

Matt: I feel like the older I get, the more respectful and the more intuitive about reading the room I get. I wish I could go back and correct a lot of errors I made in regarding human interaction.

Andrew: Yeah, and I think it is possible to sort of swing that too far the other way like, you're too worried about everybody liking you and that's not necessarily what's going to make the best record. I just can't be the kind of person who feels like you need to make somebody hate you. I actually heard somebody say if they were doing vocals and they didn't make them cry, they weren't doing their job. Well, that just seems crazy to me. That's not the way I want to do it. I err on the side of wanting people to enjoy being in the room with me.

One of the things in my career is, I don't know that I've made every band's most successful record, but I've made a lot of records that the bands say are their favorite records. That's to me what the job is. I don't know what a hit is. I can't pretend to know, so I would much rather that we get to the end of a project and love it for all the right reasons and then just see how it goes.

Matt: Obviously you've had many years of experience. You mentioned your 10,000 hours, your Malcolm Gladwell reference there, I like that. Let's talk a little bit about advice. First of all, advice to the up-and-coming crowd who really wants to get into this world, and, second, advice to guys like me who are already in it and have experience, but who really want to excel and take it up a notch.

Andrew: Yeah, it's tough man. In terms of specifically doing this or that, I don't know that I'll come up with anything. I think something that's really important, though, is to only get into it because it is your passion and you can't *not* do it. If you think like, "Oh, it'll be cool," or, "Yeah, I'll make some money," or, "I've heard they do blow during the sessions, and I like that," just go do blow then. Don't do this, because it's really, really difficult. There are a million people who want to do it.

There are a bunch of people better than you who are going to be less successful than you. There are a bunch of people much worse than you who will be way more successful than you, and that's just the way it works. It's a very bizarre, lottery–based system, and there's no knowing anything. So, you've got to recognize that going in and embrace it and not fight it.

In terms of something a little bit more specific, I think there's a lot of people who feel as though if they could just get this one more piece of gear or this one plug-in, then they'd be able to do better work. Then their mixes would finally sound like Serban Ghenea or whatever, and that is 100 percent bullshit.

I was terrified of going in the box because I thought I'm not going to be able to make it sound good. And then I talked to Tchad Blake about it. I didn't ask him about the mixing in the box part because all it took was making the realization, Tchad is mixing in the box and has been for years and I still love the way he makes records sound. For me, I feel as though my mixes feel good, I'm not positive if they sound good or not, but I love the way his mixes sound, period.

And there are people who argue that it sounded better when he was on the console. Maybe it does, maybe it doesn't; I still think they sound amazing. He's in the box; therefore, I no longer have any excuse that I can make. And it isn't because I don't know what plug-ins he uses. He said something like when he does the Mix with the Masters, he would love for somebody to give him a song he's never heard before and say, "You can only use this EQ plug-in, this compression plug-in, and this distortion plug-in. You get three plug-ins, that's it, go mix the song."

He wants to have limitations on his tool set and he wants the challenge of finding something new. I'm not quite like that. I mean, I love exploring and finding stuff, but once I find things that work, I love the fact that I've always got it in my template and it's sort of like that's my security blanket. So, I can hear a sound in my head and I don't have to remember how to make it, I'm just like, "Oh right, that's the thing that I called this." And there are quite a few chains in my template. I don't even remember what they are and it doesn't matter to me. I don't care because they're this magic box that does the thing I want.

So, you have got to stop worrying about what gear you've got, what software you're using, where you're working, what speakers you've got. Just be in a room that doesn't sound terrible with either a pair of headphones or a pair of speakers that you know. Learn how this stuff translates, and use your ears. Nobody cares what you did to make it sound the way it sounds. All they care about, and all they'll ever know about it, is what comes out of the speakers.

If you're worried about doing something that maybe you think isn't the right way to do it but it sounds right to you, then you're thinking inside out. You have to do what sounds good to you and that's it. And if you just do that, I think there are actually a lot of people who say they want to do this and they'll turn out, they have absolutely no idea what they want it to sound like. At that point, maybe you're not doing the right thing.

You have to have some vision of what you want to come out of the speakers. Not specifically sonically, but just like, "Oh my God, I know how I want this song to feel." When you listen to it, that's all you're trying to do—and it's so easy to lose sight of it. I could go on and on and just keep saying the same thing over and over, but I think that that's really, really important.

Matt: I'm excited because everything you just said I 100 percent agree with, even down to the point of talking about the desire to, "Oh, if I only get this extra piece of gear." People who listen to the podcast know I've said that a million times. And that philosophy can financially devastate an engineer over time because they think, "Oh, if I get this," and then, "Oh, if I get this." They end up eating up any of the money that they've made because they just keep buying shit.

Andrew: And not to mention the fact, all they're really doing is making an excuse for why they don't like their own work and they're not actually trying to get better. They just stop because they say,

"Well, it's because I don't have this piece of gear." Well at that point, you're not even doing your job anymore.

Matt: Another thing you said, you said it doesn't matter what you use, it's how it turns out. I always say as long as the meal tastes good, do you give a shit if somebody cooked it on a gas stove or an electric stove in iron pots or a tin pot?

Andrew: No, not at all. And as a mixer, you've got to realize that is the deal. You're only cooking the ingredients that they gave you. You can certainly blame a terrible mix on a terrible song or something that's horribly recorded, but.... For instance, I made something recently where I'm not in love with the way the recording sounds, but I still made it feel really good. The band loves it and I've accomplished my task.

It would've been so easy to say, "Well, this will never sound good because of the way it was tracked," but that's just a cop out. Then you need to just not take the gig. You can't take the gig and then have an excuse as to why you didn't do good work.

Matt: Do these things that we've talked about for the entry–level person apply as well to the mid–level person?

Andrew: Yeah, I think it always applies. I think it's, make sure that you've got something special about what you do. Like for me, it was always that I could do multiple things. I'm also fortunate that I grew up playing trumpet, of all things, but I can read a score, I can talk music to people in any genre. Also, I spent a lot of time doing programming.

I just bought Live finally because I feel like I need to learn it because it's such a different paradigm for making music, but I understand how to program drums. I can get a synth sound. I love my modular synth. I understand synthesis. I know how the gear I'm using works. So be knowledgeable and study your craft.

But if you can have some special things about what you do, then that's a reason for people to differentiate you from somebody else because there are a million people who are really good at what we do. And like I said before, it's not even necessarily you being good at it that's going to get you a gig—it's the luck of the draw, it's who you know, it's whatever it is.

I've obviously been incredibly fortunate. I've been in the right place at the right time a bunch of times, but I've put myself in lots of places at lots of times and some of them have worked out better than others. That's just the way that works. You just have to work hard and try and be good at it. I think that will eventually win out.

Another thing is—in the same way that you shouldn't blame the gear for your lack of success or whatever it is—I think also it's easy when you feel like you're really good and let's say you're in a secondary market so you don't have some opportunities for some of the bigger records and it seems like all of the big bands from your area are working with other people. Well, don't always lust after a level of work you don't have. Find the best of the level of work you do have.

Find bands that are in the same point in their career that you are in yours, and then you can get a great reciprocal relationship where if you do something cheap you don't feel like you're being screwed because you know exactly what situation the band is in. You'll feel more ownership for it. There are a million ways to keep yourself motivated, and I think that's really the key to it because there's no telling what is going to lead to what and what is the right thing and what's the wrong thing. But other than "don't be a dick," it's hard to be specific about it.

Matt: No, I think "don't be a dick" is overall good advice in everything.

Andrew: Yes, that's going to be my new Twitter hashtag. I actually use Twitter.

Matt: #DontBeADick.

Andrew: Yup.

Matt: Andrew, thank you so much for taking the time. I know you're a busy guy and I just have to say, you're one of the nicest guys on this level that I have ever had the honor of knowing and calling a friend. I appreciate you being on here.

Andrew: Well thanks man, I really appreciate that. I really do try and live by the don't be a dick thing. I really try, and I fail. I fail, but I'm always aware of when I've failed so, yeah. But I really appreciate that. That's awesome and I love that you're doing this. This is great and it's such a great list of people you've had on it too. It's not the usual same guys who do all of the stuff. Some people I wasn't really aware of, so it's awesome.

Matt: The usual suspects, yeah. Well, I just go with people I know and people I enjoy talking with. People who I have questions that it gives me an excuse to go, "Let me call Andrew and bug him."

Andrew: I think it's super important the way the industry is now. You're not going to go be an assistant and have an apprenticeship anymore. You've got to learn on your own, and the way you do it is your podcast, Pensado's Place, Mix With the Masters. It's a new way of learning it, and it's really, really important.

Matt: All right Andrew, you take care and thanks again.

Andrew: OK, thanks man.

# Kim Rosen

## Backstory and Introduction

I can't recall who it was that recommended I interview mastering engineer Kim Rosen for the podcast—in those first couple years of Working Class Audio, my organization skills were seriously a work in progress. I do remember by the end of the original interview feeling a bond with Kim not only because of our mutual love of audio but also because of the fact we are both parents. Audio professionals who are parents have two main loves in their lives to talk about, commiserate over, tell stories of, and share tips on.

Since the airing of the original interview, Kim and I have worked together on a couple of records, with me mixing and her mastering. She is fantastic at what she does and I love her work.

Kim has mastered records for some amazing artists, including Bonnie Raitt, Aimee Mann, The Milk Carton Kids, Emmylou Harris, Steve Earle, and Kris Kristofferson. Three of the records she has mastered have been nominated for Grammys, with one of those (Aimee Mann's *Mental Illness*) winning for Best Folk Album in 2017.

Kim's professional work continues to expand into the world of gear. At NAMM in 2018, Kim and her amazing husband Dave gave a sneak peak at the first product from their new company, Whitestone Audio, which was officially announced at AES 2018. Her approach to the work/life balance is inspirational and serves as an example of how to succeed in today's landscape.

Enjoy.

-Matt

# Interview with Kim Rosen

Matt: Welcome to the podcast and thanks for taking the time to do this. So you're from North Hampton, Massachusetts. But you live in Ringwood, New Jersey now.

Kim: Yeah, it's about 45 minutes from New York City, so we're close enough to get in there if we need to but we're far enough away that I live around a lot of trees and on a lake. I get to look outside my window and have a little bit of peace, outside the mayhem of the studio. We're not that far from the city but we feel a world away.

## Mastering and Good Customer Service

Matt: I read your interview in *Tape Op*. The guy that you interned for originally, Allen Douches—it was really interesting to read how he was writing down every single detail of what to do in Pro Tools for you and how after you got into some tracking sessions, you realized that maybe mastering was more your thing.

Kim: You know, when he hired me, he wanted an intern for his mastering studio. But he also happened to have an engineer, a young engineer, that he had worked with for years who was doing tracking in his mastering studio at night. Even though he hired me to be an intern and to train to help him with production duties for mastering, he also wanted me to be exposed to all kinds of engineering because I had no experience. I didn't really know what I was interested in yet. It could have been possible that mastering wasn't for me. Maybe I was more interested in doing tracking, and the only way to figure that out was to do it. That's kind of why I fell into helping out and assisting on some recording sessions.

The production side of mastering, and the training that he gave me for that, was pretty interesting. He was writing down how to use key commands when I didn't even know where to go to find it in the Pro Tools menu with a mouse. That's how disconnected it was. After a while, of course, you get that, but in the beginning, I just did what he told me to do until I worked a lot and I had a better idea of why I was doing what I was doing.

Matt: So did you decide that you didn't want to be a tracking engineer?

Kim: Yeah, it was this first session and I was working a late night with this young band, with a young engineer, and they were pretty unruly. I know better, and I have far more knowledge of how sessions work these days, but at the time, being involved in it and trying to help set up mics and getting sounds before we record and watching the dynamic of the band and getting them focused—right off the bat, I knew I didn't want to deal with that. If I want to deal with audio and I want to do something in audio, I want to work with *audio*, I don't want to be distracted by people.

Matt: It can be off-putting, I will say. I've done some sessions where I've thought, why am I here?

Kim: Again, it was a young band, so it was obviously not the best example that I could be exposed to, but of course I knew that if I really was interested in tracking and recording that that's where you start. You start off with bands that are at your level, and they might not be the best, most professional, most polished group of guys or girls, and you just have to work with what you're given. I knew pretty quickly that that just wasn't going to fit with my personality, you know? Someone who wants to record, you have the drive and the dedication to do it no matter what. You'll overcome the energy and the drama of the band because you love it so much. But for me, right away, I was able to say, yeah, not so much. Let me focus on mastering. Let me really get into what is going on here and see if that's a better fit for me.

Matt: As a mastering engineer, do you ever get audio that you hope is going to be great, but instead it's just garbage? Do you ever stop and say to the mix engineer, have you considered remixing this?

Kim: No. Not specifically those words. I will take a much different approach to asking, a different way that's worked for me over the years. I'll ask the client, "Tell me how you feel about your mixes. Tell me what you're hoping to get from mastering. Tell me if there's something that you were unable to do in mixing that you were hoping I could help you with in mastering." I try not to say, "This is garbage; you should remix." I try to really be accepting of what they're giving me.

Maybe it is the best they can do. Maybe they don't have a good engineer that's working with them. Maybe they're doing this themselves, and maybe they really think that what they've done is pretty good. I don't want to, I don't know, *shame* them because they don't have a lot of talent but they still want to go through this process. I'll try to be provocative and ask them questions about how they feel about it. So then I can pose the question, "Well this is what I'm hearing in the mixes. This is what I'm dealing with in mastering. Let me give you a couple of initial masters. You can listen to them and see how you feel the mastering has worked, if it's improved what you've wanted to."

I try to make it more of a process as opposed to, "Meh, you really should remix this." Because they wouldn't be coming to me if they had a better option. If they're ready to master and they're done with their mixing, I try to accept that this is what it is. I will ask if slight mix changes can be made, but I cannot recall any occasion where I would say, "Guys, this really isn't up to par. I think you need to remix this whole thing before you bring it in for mastering."

Matt: You'd make a good doctor for somebody who's walking into the doctor's office in an unhealthy state. How do you feel about your weight or your diet? Is that working for you?

Let's say you get a flawed mix, maybe from a band who does their own recording, and you tighten it up, make it sound commercially competitive, and hand it back to them. They then listen to your mastering job on the same system they mix on, and they start to give you pointers. They'll say it sounds great but ask you to, basically, take the reverse of the EQ curve of the whole track and try to bring it back to the knuckle–head state it was in? Does that happen?

Kim: It does happen. I'll get EQ notes from clients. I'll give them a master and they'll come back and they'll say, "I really like the mastering. It sounds great but I popped on an EQ, and I made some adjustments, and here are the notes. Do you think you can make that change for me?" Those are the moments when I'm thinking in my head, OK, well I can do this for them, or I can use it as an opportunity to have a conversation with them like "OK, your doing this EQ makes it sound better to you; what was bothering you about the mastering I gave you?" Sometimes I can achieve a sound a client wants without doing what they're telling me to do, and I don't know if that makes sense. Sometimes a client will tell me, "I don't want you to add top end" or "I don't want you to take away the low end." There might be too much low end in the mix, and I'll use some other way to not EQ it out but just control it more.

When a client sends me specific notes like that, I try to be accommodating because this is a customer-service-oriented business after all. I try to do it in a way where we're still collaborating. Or maybe someone will just say, "I just want it brighter." Instead of using their specific EQ notes, I then will go and do what I think works to make it brighter. I might not necessarily use their notes, but I'll do what I think will make it sound the way they want. It doesn't happen often, but when it happens it's kind of that voice in your head—"Well, then why don't *you* master the record?" But you just need to stop and figure out, OK, well how can we communicate and still let me do my job but really give the artist what they want.

Matt: Do you ever give an artist what they want and not feel confident that what you gave them is the right thing? Do you ever feel awkward like, "I don't know if I want my name on that one"?

Kim: Maybe not so much "I don't want my name on that," but definitely—and most specifically with clients who really want a loud album. There are many, many times—and I'm sure many, many mastering engineers will agree with this and will have experienced the same thing—you'll make something loud, and you'll send it to the client. They'll listen to it and they'll say, "Great, sounds great. Can you make it louder?" Of course, I can make it louder but the question is, will it sound good? "Don't care, make it louder."

I find myself still saying, OK, well, customer service, and I will do it and I will send it out. Man, that previous version was just so much better in so many ways, but the client is ready to move forward with this loudest, louder, crazy version. That happens, not so much lately, but over the years that has really been the hardest thing to let go and let the client direct how loud, how insanely loud, they want their project to be. It's never ever something I wouldn't want my name on. I'm proud of everything that I've worked on and proud of being able to work with a client to give them what they want.

Matt: What drives you nuts about mix engineers in what they give you?

Kim: There's really only two things that routinely jump out to me. Too much low end—so too much kick drum, too much bass guitar. Or too much top end—too much cymbals, too much EQ on the mix bus or anywhere on the mix, you know?

More than anything, it's the low end more than the top end. When I start having to use EQ to kind of sculpt out and tame the low end, there's all these frequencies that may have been recorded on the vocal that, even down at a frequency where I'm only dealing with the low end, there's still frequencies down there that give weight and depth and warmness to vocals, to guitars, so that if I'm EQ'ing out for bass guitar and kick drum, even slightly, I'm going to end up with a loss up there, and the top end starts sounding thinner. I'm speaking in small amounts, but for me, in my ears, when I'm working and I start to hear

*"When I start having to use EQ to kind of sculpt out and tame the low end... there's still frequencies down there that give weight and depth and warmness to vocals, to guitars, so that if I'm EQ'ing out for bass guitar and kick drum, even slightly, I'm going to end up with a loss up there, and the top end starts sounding thinner."*

things being taken away from the mid-range and the top end, it just kind of bums me out because then it's a lot more work to get everything back once I'm working on taming the low end.

I'm talking about three, four dB of cut in EQ. I'm not talking about minimal stuff. Minimal stuff with sculpting low end is pretty routine in mastering, but when I have to make larger adjustments is when I start to lose things in the mix that I wish I didn't have to. That's an occasion when I would ask the client if they could make a mix change, to give me a mix with a little less kick, a little less bass guitar. And most of the time, mix engineers are just like, sure. Then there's the 25 percent of the time where the band is just like, "No, we paid the mix engineer. We don't have any money to get any revisions made. Can you just use it the way it is?"

## Business Collaboration

Matt: As far as the range of your business that comes to you, sometimes you have bands coming at you to ask you to master and sometimes you have mix engineers, I would assume, kind of acting as the liaison. Can you give me a range of what percentage of that is the case? Is it 60/40 in favor of engineers or bands?

Kim: I would say 60/40 engineer to band. There are also times where bands will contact me because they are working with an engineer that I've worked with before and they recommended me. I might not be dealing with the engineer but it's someone I've worked with multiple times and they referred the band to me. The engineer is not the liaison but they are the catalyst to put me in touch with this client, this band. Most of the time when I'm working with engineers that I work with on a regular basis, those aren't really occasions where I'm having issues with the mix.

When I'm having that 40 percent of a band that heard from another band or that checked out my website and saw my credits and dropped me a line because they want to work with me, those might be more of the occasions where I have issues with the mix. There's more of a back and forth and a conversation about getting things right. Making things sound good. If I'm working with an engineer that I've worked with a lot, then a lot of the issues that I have, they're just not there. We've worked together so much that the process has been streamlined. They know what to give to me. I know what I'm going to be getting and it's a lot easier and more enjoyable to work with.

Matt: Interesting. As we're having this conversation I'm thinking, it seems like there's a lot of isolation and segmentation for all of us. So like a band will seek out the cheapest mix engineer they can find and then they'll get what they need from them. Then they'll go shopping for a mastering engineer. I almost see a need for a tag team approach, where somebody would approach me, and I could say, "Yeah, I can mix your record and have it mastered with so-and-so," team up with a mastering engineer like you, where I can quote one price and say, "Yeah, we can get everything done for this much, and I'll handle this part of it. Kim will handle this part of it and give you your master." Do you ever do that?

Kim: I do have a setup with a studio in Nashville, Welcome to 1979.

Matt: Chris Mara's place.

Kim: Yep. They approached me a couple of years ago. They had been working with an engineer, and they really wanted to grow that business, the mastering side of it. We came to an agreement where they advertise mastering on their website, and people who go to the 1979 website, they can book mastering, and it gets sent over to me. They try to encourage the clients who are in there recording and mixing to have their mastering done with me. Then the client will deal with them for billing on their end, and it becomes a more simplified, straightforward approach for people to go through that way. It's really great for me, because I really enjoy them. They're great people, and all the stuff they send my way is fantastic.

As a business owner, I'm always looking for ways to expand my business and get more clients. It's been really great, and we continue to work together that way. As a matter of fact, I just mastered something yesterday, a single at 192kHz, and sent that back to them.

They take care of everything for me: the billing and everything. We just take care of the accounting side separately. It's really painless, and wonderful, and it's great to work with them. But that's really the only occasion where it's streamlined financially. Most other occasions where I work with an engineer who likes to try to get the client to master with me, it's still billed separately. They will do their billing through me. I take care of that separately. They will have paid their mix engineer, and then I'll bill them myself.

## Mastering for Vinyl

Matt: Welcome to 1979 cuts vinyl, so I assume you send in vinyl masters for them to cut from. Can you discuss the differences between mastering for vinyl versus mastering for a digital release, whether that's CD or a download? What is it that most young, up–and–coming engineers don't realize and that they should know?

Kim: Well it's certainly something that I didn't know until I really started working more closely with Cameron, who does all the lacquer cutting at 1979. When I was working at the studio I used to work at, when I was training, I was taught to use CD masters, the same files, if you were sending for vinyl. That's what I did. It wasn't until I really started talking with Cameron about it, and when we started working together, the first thing I did, they just had me remaster something that was already done on their side, but I mastered it. Then they had Cameron cut a reference lacquer and I listened to it, and I was like, "Wow."

Really for the first time, I was able to hear where I could have made improvements to how I mastered, and the master that I gave them, to really make the vinyl shine. There are several changes that I now make because of that. I certainly roll off a little bit of low end for vinyl masters, depending on the music. Routinely, I would say from about 80 hertz, I might put a shelf filter on, and take down a half dB, which might not seem like a lot, but if it's pretty straightforward, not too loud, crazy stuff, that's enough. Cameron will take care of putting all the low–end information into mono, so I don't need any elliptical filter craziness on that.

Then I'll head to the top end. A lot of times they're really kind of standard... maybe not top end so much—maybe I just end up making a master that's not as loud. Maybe a half dB to a dB of less volume will also help bring down the top end. These are standard changes that I will make.

Of course if I have a CD master, it's different. I had one recently that was very, very loud, insanely loud, insane amounts of low end, and I had to make pretty big changes for the vinyl master, to make it more appropriate to cut, and actually it was something that went to Cameron. He called me. He was just like, "Hey, this is crazy. Is there any way for you to make more changes?" I actually had to change it, make a couple of revisions to it, because it was kind of out of control.

Matt: Oh, wow.

Kim: But standard changes would be a little less volume, a half to one dB, bring down the low end. Most of the stuff that I master tends not to be too bright, so I don't really tame the top end too much. You could have a really long conversation about all the ways that you can tweak and change vinyl depending on how long the side of the record is—like changing the sequence to put a softer song at the end of a side.

Matt: Vinyl obviously is gaining market share, very little, but it's still gaining regardless. For those who don't know, what should mix engineers be aware of when they're mixing projects that will end up on vinyl?

Kim: If a mix engineer was making something that was strictly going to vinyl, they really need to be careful of low–end information that is off to the sides. If there's too much low end on the sides, it won't play back well, so it really needs to be more in the center. I know that Cameron tries to put it to mono. That is one big thing. Then a lot of top end, again, like very bright top end, won't play back well, it will sound maybe distorted.

But other than that, I really don't think that as a mix engineer there's too much that you need to be careful with. What you get into trouble with is more in mastering. It can't be too loud. That's one physical limitation of vinyl that you can't get around. The amount of space on a record is the amount of space on a record.

## The Mastering Room, Home, and Family

Matt: I understand you built your mastering room off the side of your house, after having been mastering inside your house.

Kim: Yes.

Matt: Can you elaborate a little bit on cost?

Kim: Yeah, that's hard, because it wasn't just an addition for the studio. We bought this house. It was an 800 square foot log cabin. We bought the house knowing that we wanted to build on for living space. We never intended to add a mastering room, but when I left the studio I was working at, I had just had my first child. He was a few months old. I started working right away. But when we started to move forward with the plans for the addition, we were like, "Well, we need to make a mastering room now. I can't continue to work in the living room." The cost of the room was probably minimal in the scope of what we spent on the addition, because we gave ourselves a whole new house and a lot of stress.

It's still a modest-sized house. My room here is only 14 by 25, the mastering room. I suppose we doubled the size of our original house. Everything else is still pretty modest. We renovated the kitchen, renovated the bathroom, added a bedroom, and just living space, but the mastering room itself was a no-brainer add-on to it.

Matt: I have to say you are the first mom we've had on, though we've had a lot of dads, and I'm a father. So you work from home. If I may ask, how old are your kids?

Kim: My kids are three and six. My six-year-old is in first grade and my three-year-old goes to daycare.

Matt: OK.

Kim: So I get my time to work all day. If I really think back to the beginning when I had an infant and how much I worked prior to having kids, anybody who's an engineer knows how much time you put into being available whenever and how that directly relates to success and moving forward with your career. I don't really feel that there would have been any other way for me to continue to work as much as I've worked as a mastering engineer if I didn't do it at home. Working this way really enables me to be available whenever, to take opportunities for clients and projects that come here and want to work with me. I can work overnight if I need to and I want to work. Being able to have my studio at home, it just makes it so much easier to do that.

Matt: It really does. I work from home and it allows me to be the one in the family to go and drop off and pick up the kids, and really take that load off my wife's shoulders so that she can do her job, which is a more corporate job. Obviously, we're both benefiting from living in the 21st century and being able to shift files back and forth across the world without a lot of hassle. It's an amazing thing. And it allows us, I think—and I'm sure you would agree—it allows us to be the parents that we want to be. Which is really, really nice.

Kim: Totally. I enjoy having my kids around where I work. I have a dog too. It's all just here. They see what I do. They still don't really understand it. I'm pretty sure that they think that I master every artist I play in the car, which is just not true. Especially when they ask me to play Katy Perry or something like that. But I try to explain otherwise.

Matt: My kids always ask me, "Dad did you play drums on this or did you mix this?"

Kim: It's great to be able to do the parent stuff when it needs to be done. I'll be honest, there are lots of times where I'm trying to make a deadline or I'm really in it on a project and trying to get stuff done or problem–solve and my husband works, and I have to stop what I'm doing and go get my kids. It might not be the best time to be doing this and I really should be staying here and doing what needs to get done, but if I don't go pick up my child then they're going to get left there by themselves.

Sometimes it becomes this really crazy back and forth balance. My husband is amazing with picking up the slack and helping out, but we're both really busy with our careers. We're at a tipping point where it would be great if I could get a little bit of help, take a little pressure off of me, because even though I have a demanding job and he has a demanding job, a lot of times I'm the one to do all the kid stuff because I'm mom and that's what kids want sometimes.

Matt: I have two boys, seven and nine. The seven-year-old loves to play the game Connect 4. I have to just tell you he's a badass. I have lost to him so many times, it's ridiculous. I'll be in the middle of mixing and I think, OK, they're either doing their homework, playing with one another, or playing a game, or they're occupied. And then the door opens, and I'm in the middle of something, and I get, "Dad, will you play Connect 4 with me? My brother won't play with me right now." I'm like "Ahhh, OK."

Kim: Mm-hmm.

Matt: I've given up. I'm like, "I'm going to do it. I'm going to go play Connect 4 right now."

Kim: I can't even keep track of the number of times… As great as it is, kids go to school. Sometimes kids are home sick. And I find myself working at home when the kids are sick. The big joke between my husband and I is that our kids, when they're home, they are like garbage disposals. They continuously eat. So I'll be sitting here working. I will have come in after breakfast and sat down with my coffee and I'm working for 20 minutes. Only 20 minutes, set the kid up with TV, which is another thing that my children do a lot of is watching TV while I work. Twenty minutes I'll be working and one of the children will come in, "Can I have something to eat?" "We just finished breakfast 20 minutes ago. No, go watch your movie." And they'll go and they'll be back 20 minutes later, "Can I have something to eat?" It becomes this big joke. That that's all they want. I'm trying to manage working, and listening, and constantly being interrupted, and sometimes you've just got to get up and feed your kid.

Matt: Sometimes you just got to stop mastering a record.

Kim: That's right.

Kim: It gets a little crazy around here. Someone's delivering something. The dog is barking. My phone is ringing. I got to talk to a client. The kids are here. It gets a little hectic sometimes but we try to embrace it and just try not to hide what we are because everybody's working. It's not a matter of trying to be rude, or trying not to be rude, or trying to be something that we're not.

We're a couple with a family, running a business and that's also a whole other avenue on why I love my clients and why I love doing this because the people that I work with, they're just really cool. Everybody understands and feels good about talking with me. Everybody just gets along and we're all living our life and being real people and it's not just this corporate machine. It's really nice to interact with people who think about audio the same way, think about music, love music the same way that we do because that's why we do this. We love music. That's how I met my husband.

He was thrilled when we started my own mastering room. He used to play in bands but he has become my business partner in running this mastering studio. He does things like he works on my website and he helps me research gear and pick out the right kind of gear for me and for my mastering chain, but the way the partnership has turned out is pretty awesome. Being music lovers and it being such a big part of our life to be able to run a business and have me work and do what I do—it just enriches everything. It's really great.

Matt: That's fantastic. That's a level of involvement from a partner that I don't think a lot of people have, and that's a great position to be in. I love my wife. I think she's fantastic, but she's not involved in my business in that level. She's got enough on her plate so we run pretty independently.

So as a result of working at home and working where your home is located, I get that you don't have a lot of attended sessions.

Kim: No. No. I've had a couple people in here and I certainly don't discourage it, but it's just the way everything is set up these days. Maybe if I were a big facility in kind of a metropolitan hub, New York City, somewhere else more accessible, it would be easier, but I work on clients that are all over the country. It's not really a local thing, so it's harder to get people in, certainly, you got to pay to get yourselves there.

Attended mastering sessions are also kind of a different thing. I mean I love them. I haven't had an opportunity to do one in a long time. The way you interact with a client, the artist in real time, while you're working on a project is really fun, and mastering for me is about vibe. There's no better vibe than when you're sitting there with the artist, trying to bring everything to a finish. I kind of miss that, but again, which just really touches my ability to work whenever, with unattended sessions, I can shuffle my schedule around and make it work, based on what's going on here.

At any given time, I might have five to eight projects in various stages of work. I can do that because they're unattended. Some, I'm just starting. Some, I'm waiting for approval. Some, I need to get finishing. Unattended work allows me to really put things in the order that I need to get them done as efficiently and as quickly as possible for the client.

Matt: I feel like I can do my best work mixing when I don't have anybody in front of me because I'm not trying to put on a dog and pony show, and I can just go down rabbit holes and experiment and test without freaking anybody out. Do you think that that applies to mastering at all?

Kim: There is definitely something to be said for that. I mean you are right. Maybe there are moves and opportunities that I might not take if I were working on an attended session. Whether or not I would take those risks, if I was in an attended session, I suppose depends on the client. If I know them. Maybe a bit nervous working with them. So I suppose that that could be kind of a drawback to an attended session.

Matt: I mean you're at the back end of the process, and it seems that usually at mastering, everybody's always freaked out and rushing, and they just got the mixes the day before, and they've set unrealistic deadlines sometimes, whether it's with a record company or not. I don't know, man, when I mix, I'll hit a point where I have to take a break. I'm like, "Well, I'm at home. It's lunchtime. Let's do 'On Demand' with Stephen Colbert," and I'll go watch that and eat some chips and salsa and have about four more cups of coffee and then get back on the horse.

If a client's here, that's just not going to fly. That's going to make everybody feel like, "What do you mean you need to watch Stephen Colbert?"

Kim: I guess it could depend on your mood that day. I guess it depends on the music. I guess it depends on a lot of things, whether or not an attended session would hold you back. I suppose there's plenty of occasions where it might, and you might just be having one of those days where you want to just take a break and let your ears rest, and you come back to it, and you're just like, "Yeah. All right, now. I get it now. I'm back on track."

But then, I think there are also opportunities that you get with attended sessions. There are drawbacks to each, and there are pluses to each, and so if you really feel you do your best work unattended, then that's the way you should try to make it happen. But I feel like, I like being pushed out of my comfort zone. Sometimes, really magical things can happen when you're not sitting around, doing things the same way you always do, and maybe something new and different comes of it.

Yeah, so I like being efficient and doing what works, but I also like taking the occasional risk and doing something a little bit different.

## Retirement and Financial Planning

Matt: If you're cool with it, I'd like to speak on maybe the topic of retirement savings and financial stuff. I don't know if that's an awkward question. Is that something you're on top of, or…?

Kim: That's a great question. When I started working at the studio I used to work at, my old boss and his wife, her parents sold life insurance. They were all about planning. I was 23, and I was like, "If I'm going to be in this industry for a long time, I'm never going to have a 401K. I should start thinking about doing something for retirement now." And so what they got me into was a whole life insurance policy. That's something that's going to grow and grow, and based on pretty modest monthly premiums that I've been paying since I was 23, so that's 12 years. By the time I'm ready to retire, it's this life insurance policy that I can borrow against and use it like a retirement fund.

If by the time I'm ready to retire, it's worth $800,000, that's the value of the life insurance policy, I can borrow against it as I want or take money out of it, and it just reduces the benefit that my family gets, should I expire or die or whatever. That is the only thing that I have set up. Maybe it's given me this false idea that I have something reliable planned. I certainly should and would like to make some more moves to save some more, but aside from that, I have not done anything. But I'm still proud that I at least did that because I know that when most people are 23, the last thing they're worried about is retirement.

Matt: It's interesting, though. I think that in our industry, you could get away with working longer. Look at the longevity of people like Al Schmitt, Glyn Johns, and Leslie Ann Jones. The older you get, people look at you and go, "Oh, they're the great wizards in our world. They're the Yodas." People tend to have respect, whereas I think in the tech world, you get to around 50, 55, people start to go, "Hmm." I don't know if you're familiar with the movie *Logan's Run*, but the people in that movie had a little marble–like thing embedded in their hand, and it had a light. When that light went out, at the age of 30, you were killed. The whole movie is based on the idea that Logan and his crew are running because their lights are going out. They're turning 30 or something, and it's ridiculous. It's a hilarious older sci-fi movie.

I just think, "Man, you know what? I'm going to do audio as long as somebody will write me a check, and I can hear."

Kim: I guess that's the most important factor is as long as you can hear. I mean I would feel the same way. First of all, I can't believe that I'm doing this. I mean becoming a mastering engineer isn't something that was a dream of mine since I was young, and yet I can't imagine doing anything else. I can't imagine having any other career, and I have no desire to have any other career. I am excited by the idea of working more and more for many years. You make your own schedule when you're an engineer, and you only take on projects that you agree to. So even when you're not retired, you can take off and go travel with your spouse or your friends.

Matt: Yeah, what's not to like about that?

Kim: You can partially retire, but certainly, planning financially so that you have the ability to do that is just as important as having the desire not to fully retire at 65 or 70 or whenever people tend to want to retire.

## Networking, Friendship, and Credibility

Matt: You seem to really enjoy what you do, and you have a passion for it, obviously. Your body of work looks pretty large, so it doesn't look like you're a fly–by–night operation by any stretch. You seem to have made some really good alliances with the folks at Welcome to 1979. By the way, how did that come about? With you in New Jersey and them in Nashville?

Kim: This is, will be a long answer, but it will make sense, I promise. When I started my own space, I was really kind of shell–shocked. It was really kind of all of a sudden. I really didn't have an intention of starting my own place, but I found myself in a position where that's what I was going to do. When I started mastering in my living room, very shortly after that, I was kind of feeling like, "Yeah, I'm here. I'm doing this, but I don't have my own audio family and my own friends. My own little network." I'm doing this on my own. I kind of felt like I needed to get something else here. Right at that time, my husband, who does graphic design, was put in touch with a guy named Gil Griffith. He runs Wave Distribution.

Matt: Oh, yeah. I've met Gil.

Kim: He lives one town over from us. We made friends with Gil and started hanging out and spending time and meeting up. Gil has this great network around him. We've become friends with Dave Derr of Empirical Labs and Kooster McAllister, who works at Record Plant Remote. I kind of built up this little family of people involved in audio, and I started to feel great. Now, I'm not so alone.

One of the people Gil introduced us to was Chris Mara. We met Chris and his wife Yoli, and they're fantastic. They're also a couple running a business. They have young kids. It was something we had in common. We just hit it off. Chris came up with the idea of a partnership and doing the mastering.

Really, just the getting out part and meeting people and putting myself out there, which was kind of hard initially because

*"I really felt kind of like, 'Do I belong here? Do I have enough credits? Am I credible enough to be out here saying I'm a mastering engineer?' I was kind of insecure at first."*

starting my own room and starting off mastering on my own, I really felt kind of like, "Do I belong here? Do I have enough credits? Am I credible enough to be out here saying I'm a mastering engineer?" I was kind of insecure at first. But once I started getting out and meeting people and continuing to work and work and work, that kind of faded away. Now, it's like you meet people who are like-minded, who, as I mentioned before, love music the way that I do, who think about music the way that I do, and it's really cool.

A lot of friendships and the partnerships that I made by going out and meeting people in audio conventions have been so lucrative—lucrative as friendships and lucrative as working together from a business standpoint.

Matt: That's very cool. I have to say I think that a lot of people feel insecure if they don't have major label credits. I'm just here to say that's bullshit. I feel that you don't have to have major label credits to be a legitimate commodity. Now, maybe that looks better for the gear manufacturers in the endorsement deals. I think that you could still be a working–class person who does a great job who doesn't work necessarily on the latest pop star that comes out of wherever, or a country star.

Kim: Right. The best way to learn how to master is just to master. I understand it's hard to find clients and to get people to trust you to master, but the more you work, the better you get. It wasn't so much not having major label credits for me. I look back now, and I see, I've worked on a lot of projects. The best way for me to feel credible now is to go back and listen to them. Nearly every single project that I could go back and listen to that I've worked on—I'm proud of every single one of them. Even the ones that might not sound that great, from early on in my career. I'm still really proud of it. I feel so lucky. All the music that I work on, I connect to it. I love it. It really becomes something that I'm proud of. And what is credibility anyway? I could say that I don't feel credible because I don't like talking gear because that's not my thing, because for me, it's how I hear. It's the music. It's the vibe. It's the work that I do. I mean the best way for me to show a client what I do is to do a test master for them. Let you hear. Me explaining what I do or why I might be better than a different engineer is going to do nothing. Let me just show you. That's really, for me, that's the way that I explain or speak.

Matt: You're perfectly suited for this podcast then. This has been great. I appreciate your time to sit and chat with me. I think this is good information that you've shared here. Also, it's nice to have another parent on. Kids and audio.

Kim: Sometimes, they get really sick of the songs I'm working on. I drive around with them a lot—to daycare or here or there—and I listen to my work in the car nearly all the time. They get pretty sick of me playing the same stuff over and over again sometimes. They'll just have had it. And I'll just say, "Hey. Sorry. Gotta be quiet. Time to be quiet. I gotta listen." And they do. They're pretty agreeable kids. I would say that I'm pretty lucky.

Matt: I'm always fascinated as far as the songs that my kids like. I'll play a song and listen to a mix. In my brain, I'm like making all the changes in my head, and then I'll hear, "Hey, Dad, can you play that again?"

Kim: Yes.

Matt: Like, "Oh, you like that. Well, that's good. That's good. I'll let them [the client] know that."

Kim: Yeah, they'll come running down the hallway. They'll bust open the door. They'll start dancing around in the room. I'll be like, "Oh, I guess you like this song."

Matt: It's been great meeting you and chatting with you. Thanks, Kim.

Kim: Yes. Thanks so much, Matt.

# Langston Masingale

## Backstory and Introduction

It was WCA alum Alan Evans (WCA#133) who suggested I talk with Langston Masingale, and I'm glad he did. Langston started his work in recording studios 25 years ago at age 16 in his uncle's studio in New Jersey. He went on to help start JJ Audio Mics in 2009. In 2014, he struck out on his own and invented what would become the core technology of his tape–emulation product, Zulu. He formed Handsome Audio in 2015 with his partner Tod Levine, and they officially released Zulu in the same year.

Langston still owns a recording studio, Narrative Audio, in Syracuse, New York, where he produces and records artists. His passion for the analog aesthetic drives him to create new and interesting tools for the modern recording engineer and record producer alike. He's passionate about what he does and it's clear his early exposure to analog tape has shaped his current sonic viewpoint in a world of DAWs.

Langston's passion is palpable. Some people who sell products have a snake oil salesman vibe about them, but Langston is the real deal. He believes in a certain analog aesthetic based on his early experiences, and it's almost as if he wants to share his early experiences with you by way of his products.

When I initially talked with him, I knew I was dealing with an intensely smart individual. Langston stays in touch and lets me know what he's working on next. That's one of the great bonuses of this WCA universe to me—I get to peer inside the workings of audio's brilliant minds. Langston is definitely one of those.

Enjoy!

-Matt

## Interview with Langston Masingale

Matt: Welcome to the podcast, man. It's great to have you here.

Langston: Thank you for having me.

Matt: We can definitely thank our mutual friend, Al Evans.

Langston: Yeah. Alan's awesome.

Matt: Does he like to be called Al?

Langston: I know a lot of people that do call him that, but I just call him Alan. It's one of those things where I've never been corrected. So, it's just the way that I know him. He tours under that name. I don't have any nicknames for him or anything like that. I just call him Alan.

Matt: I tend to shorten people's names. My youngest son is named Emerson, so I just call him Em.

Langston: That's a cool name.

Matt: Langston's a very cool name. I can't see calling you Lang, though.

Langston: Thank you. Yeah, you see, my name doesn't shorten well. So, what I do is just turn it into initials. So when I write people emails from Handsome Audio, I just say L. Then, everybody's like, "Thanks, L." Because my name just gets butchered. I'll tell people my name and they'll be like, "You know, Lancelot, it's just great to have you here." *Lancelot?* It just sounds like something you'd name a pimp, you know? Only pimps are getting named Lancelot these days. It's not a name you'd give a boy if you expect him to be respected and admired. It's just not the thing to do anymore. So, Langston shortens to L pretty easily, and a lot of people call me L.

Matt: It's funny, because I think, before Al said anything, I had come across the Zulu analog simulation product that you make. I don't know if that's the proper way to introduce it. But essentially, I had seen that web page before. Then, he said, "You have to talk to Langston. He's an inventor. He's a producer. He's an...." He named all these things, and I said, "I'm sold. You had me at inventor. I'm in."

Langston: Well, thank you.

## Meet Zulu

Matt: Let's start with what little I know about the Zulu. That's an interesting product on a number of levels.

Langston: Yes.

Matt: It differentiates you from many other guests, in that not many of the guests on Working Class Audio have a product like that. So, tell me about that, and tell me how it came about.

Langston: I started recording music in a family member's studio back in the early 90s. Around '93, to be exact. The thing is, in that studio, they were using Tascam machines. Like, the one-inch and two-inch machines. I was also getting some exposure to the cassette Portastudio stuff. One of the things that ingrained itself into my cognitive connection to the analog studio process was that tape had a sound. Tape had a behavior. It had, almost like, a self–awareness to it.

So, when I began tinkering with different circuitry, and different passive designs, to make what is now known as Zulu, I had heard many other things, like plug-ins and hardware. No offense to anybody else, everybody has pretty much attacked this problem.

*"One of the things that ingrained itself into my cognitive connection to the analog studio process was that tape had a sound. Tape had a behavior. It had, almost like, a self-awareness to it."*

This is one of those ongoing debates in digital now—that we are in this great, wonderful, limitless platform of recording audio, yet people still keep pushing backwards, against the advent of crystal-clear recording.

They keep trying to find ways to murk it up, to muddy it up, to dirty it up, to give them something they're more familiar with. Right? Part of the issue with that is, people go for some brute-force solution to the problem. I even had something like a Tascam 30. I had come across one on eBay, one year, for like $400, and I bought it. It was a great machine. It had a reel of Ampex 456 still on it. Pretty good calibration on most of the eight channels that were there, on the eight tracks.

This deck did stuff at each end of the spectrum, at each extreme. So, you had the less driven, less aggressive side of the spectrum where it would do something pretty cool, but the noise floor was just too bad to really use it that way. But it was a good sound. Then you had the other end of the spectrum, where, when you abused it, something musical and almost beautifully ugly happened, when you would overdrive this machine.

So it kind of occurred to me that if somebody was ever going to invent a tape simulator, it was going to require more than just tape, and the heads, and the electronics, right? There had to be some connection to the outside world. For example, whenever you use a machine like a Tascam, or an Ampex, or a Studer, or whatever you have around, you're using it with everything else you've got, too. It's like a last ditch effort, when you record to tape.

You use a compressor, to get up above the noise floor of the machine. You use an equalizer to kind of beat, and cheat, the pre-emphasis and de-emphasis circuitry that's in the tape deck. So that you don't get hiss, but you also want to beat hiss, right? So one of the ways people do it is, they pre-emphasize the tape. They boost treble. Sometimes they want some of the gel to happen in the saturation coefficient of how the tape operates, at its operating level. So you might boost a little bit of low end even more, to make the tape saturate a little earlier, based on the collective harmonic character of the source. But that all creates a relationship between the equipment that's in front of the machine and, even more so, what's after it, right?

Matt: Right.

Langston: So, most of these approaches were more of making it like a singular, self-sustaining system where the saturation does this, under these parameters, and that's it. It doesn't matter what happened before, it doesn't matter what happens after. With analog equipment, a lot of what you see, people say, "If I plug this mic into this mic preamp and this mic preamp into this compressor...." Well, in the real world, these devices, on some level, see each other, through those connections.

Tape machines are no exception to that rule; they're the same way. They have surrounding electronics, they have the actual tape process, and all of those things marry together to make something that's harmonically rich and unique. Each situation creates a myriad of variables. So my approach to Zulu was, what can I do to harness those happy accidents in a controlled way? But at the same time, I wanted to let that untamed aspect of what analog is still reign.

One of the things that I did was to not follow traditional equipment–making techniques. You have all these designs where people buffer things so that no equipment affects the other piece. What I realized was that by allowing equipment to show its true colors, by allowing them to affect each other, you're reinventing what each piece of gear was for.

So your microphone preamp became more than just a way to amplify sound, it became a way to effect change in other parts of your chain. By eliminating the technology normally used to eliminate those scenarios, we discovered that a lot of gear has hidden tones inside of it. Because we were harnessing those harmonic coefficients as part of the way to sculpt sound.

That's really what clicks in my head, with Zulu, and with tape, is that we have these controls on there that, on the surface, are just tone controls, or dynamic controls, or saturation controls. But they also are allowing Zulu to talk to what's hooked up to it, and those things also talk to Zulu. That became more of what, I felt, was more akin to how a record producer would look at a tape machine.

He or she looks at it as a piece of equipment, but also as a musical instrument. There's a great phrase that people throw around all the time in conversations, that the room is an instrument in a recording studio. My heart belongs in the world

*"So a space becomes part of the album. It isn't just where it happens. It's actually like the other member of the band. People talk about that with Sound City and The Record Plant. ...Those rooms made those albums what they were, just as much as the person behind the console."*

of tracking musicians and dealing with them and producing their records.

So a space becomes part of the album. It isn't just where it happens. It's actually like the other member of the band. People talk about that with Sound City and The Record Plant. All these other great rooms in recording history, those rooms made those albums what they were, just as much as the person behind the console.

I look at all equipment that way. That kind of means that if I'm going to embrace that philosophy, at least personally, I should be making gear that welcomes other gear to be touching it and talking to it. Rather than: "I'm here. My sound is specifically my sound, and I don't want you affecting me." But all the equipment has a mind of its own. I'm bringing that back to the table, in that conversation.

That DI box sitting on your desk, that you don't use unless somebody cuts bass, is now another tool that you can use to shape tones. That mic preamp that sits idle at mix–down, because you're not recording anything, can now be a way for you to generate some really cool sound that normally you wouldn't be able to harness digitally. There's no other piece of gear that does that, because it's not designed that way. That all revolves around my philosophy of, again, making equipment into instruments, instead of just these pieces of technology that we look at.

We look at them as soulless shapes. These things have new purposes in the world that we live in now. Simply because, I think personally, that even though digital is fantastic as far as the recall, the unlimited amounts of times you can record a take, it still lacks the soul that we miss in these old recordings. So we keep searching for that, and this is my first step in beginning that journey—with Zulu.

Matt: What's behind the name? What's the story there?

Langston: Zulu is named after the general. There's a famous general, when I was a kid, there was a movie about him called *Shaka Zulu*. He was feared, respected, and brilliant. He was unique in the way that he approached combat and also in the way that he governed. I thought about tape, in the context of the modern sense—here we are now, and tape is a dead technology, it's been abandoned on many levels, and it's not a very popular way to record for most people, mainly because of the expense, the hassle, the discipline involved, the discipline of the staff using it right.

But it's a rebellious approach to recording audio, too. It's just like J.J. Abrams, when he still cuts the 35 millimeter stock and he records *Star Wars* that way, some huge venture. He says, "I like film, because I like the way film looks. I don't care about the inconvenience, this is fantastic."

For me, people that record to analog tape, they're rebels. Shaka Zulu stood up against the greatest empire that ever graced the planet, the British Empire. At least one of the greatest, one of the most advanced, one of the most well–crafted, and well–trained military forces on the planet. Yet, here's this guy, in the middle of South Africa, fending off the British with spears and sandals. Shields made out of leather.

He gave the British a hard time. I look at tape like that, like it's the disruptor. That's what Shaka Zulu represented to me, that rebellious spirit of the analog-focused producer that is saying, "You know what? Digital is great, but it's still missing what I want, as a record producer. And I don't care if you tell me that I just don't know what I'm doing with digital. I can take a rock and skip it across a river. So, if you give me a photocopy, and it sinks, and you tell me my technique sucks, I still can get the rock, dude."

That's how I feel about analog tape. You don't have to get a degree in computer science to know how to hit signal on that thing and get back the splat on a snare drum. It's pretty simple. Hit it in the sweet spot, and it will always do it. With digital, it's a constant moving target, for a lot of us. Like, we just can't adapt, right? So, this is not even a crutch. It's literally giving you back the skill set that you already had.

It's giving you that proper tool to approach it, but that's what Shaka Zulu did, because he made new spears that were shorter and easier to stab people with. That's the same thing with Zulu. Hey, stop worrying so much about your levels to tape. This thing will absorb transients. You don't have to use some newfangled compressor just to get your levels under control. You don't have to worry about infinite headroom. You can worry about, hey, there actually is headroom, and it has a sound.

So when you go past this operating point, it changes the tone up. It actually gives you a texture to play with. Just like, if you bend a guitar string a certain way, the tone changes. Sometimes we need those limits, and sometimes we need to take on a non-standard approach to things, to actually be better creators, and better creatives. Zulu, man, represents all of that. The Zulu spirit is a big thing in African culture. Obviously, I'm African–American, right?

That is one of the greatest forces in the tales that little black boys and girls get told. Like, the greatness of this person. So, I've repurposed that name to embody the spirit of analog tape—which is also where a lot of great black music got recorded, on

*"There are many different contributors to the American songbook, but there're also many great contributors to the American record production book, as well the inventors. This is my way of pointing out to somebody who may be like me… you don't necessarily have to be a tape jockey; you could build shit."*

tape. When those reels were turning, you were getting James Brown, Ray Charles, you were getting Charlie Parker. These things were happening on tape.

So I want to reframe and re-grasp that. And also, on some level, bring that spirit back into the conversation. There are many different contributors to the American songbook, but there're also many great contributors to the American record production book, as well the inventors. This is my way of pointing out to somebody who may be like me—a little black kid from the hood that gets strong–armed into the record business—hey, you don't necessarily have to be a tape jockey; you could build shit.

If people lack a solution in a recording setting, make a better mic preamp. Invent a mic. Invent a better way to connect cables together. These things are possible for you, and by me putting a name on it that's Afrocentric, it also puts that earmark in the conversation. Hey, this guy did it, you can, too. Again, embodying that rebellious nature, that spirit, that disruption of what the status quo is. All of that is embodied in that phrase. People love it. Everybody wants to join the tribe.

Matt: Your story about Shaka Zulu and how it pertains to your philosophy around the product itself, I think that's great. I have an appreciation for those who are disruptors, and those who think outside the box. To me, what comes to mind is Steve Albini or Steve Jobs. I don't think there's any other Steves. I have an appreciation for those that push against the current. I like that a lot.

## Uncle Gabe and the Value of Mentorship

Matt: Correct me if I'm wrong, but I believe you grew up in Syracuse.

Langston: Yes, sir. Syracuse, New York.

Matt: If I'm correct, you also have an uncle that has a recording studio, or had a recording studio—

Langston: In New Jersey.

Matt: OK. Is he much, much older than you?

Langston: Yeah, Gabe was, like, in his 30s when I started working with him. I was just a snot-nosed teenager.

Matt: OK.

Langston: He was still a younger, handsome–looking fellow, but he just didn't age. He had that Peter Pan gene. Yeah, he was much smarter and older than I was at the time. The difference between 16 and 30, sometimes, is not so obvious, until you see maturity strike. And a 16-year-old's maturity level versus a 30-year-old man, is pretty different. That's why he was the boss man and I was the assistant.

Matt: How did he influence you?

Langston: Well, the way it works with Gabe, right, one of the most important things he ever did for me was, he took it away. What I mean by that is he let me see what a session really looked like. There was some crazy band in there from Jersey. Like hair whipping back and forth, real hardcore rock music. He let me see that and see the reaction of the band listening to themselves. He was great at what he did, man. His techniques were nuts, and people would come to him.

It was different for me to see that. Where I grew up there was a lot of diversity in my community, but not when it came to the tech side of things, unfortunately. So to see somebody that looked like me being spoken to as if he was the man—and it was in a recording studio, it's the entertainment industry—it was uplifting and inspirational.

*"...One of the most important things he ever did for me was, he took it away."*

Also, it made me want to be like him. Then he took it away. He said, "OK. Now that you see what you could be doing, you can't have it." I was like, "Well, what do I got to do to get it back?" He's like, "You see that book over there on the table?" I was like,

"Yeah." He's like, "It's 300 pages long. Read it, come back to me, and recite it to me. Show me what you know."

It was the service manual for the studio's deck. I read that thing from cover to cover, over and over again. It just consumed me; I was not going to be shot down. That thing taught me so much about electronics. It taught me about the discipline that people have that work on equipment. The care that's needed to maintain it.

All of those things became part of my upbringing as a recording studio personality, and as a recording engineer, as a person that maybe lacked a little bit of humility, like a lot of teenagers do. We lack humility. We're coming up, we think we are great, before we even are good.

Matt: Oh, yeah.

Langston: It humbled me. I mean, that's one of the biggest influences he had on me, because after that, I realized I like manuals. I used to read the manual for everything before I'd even think about buying it. Like, if there was some new drum machine. Gabe did a lot of hip-hop in his studio. He did a lot of dance music that involved drum programming. He had those Akai MPC60s there. All the Korg wonderful gadgets, et cetera, et cetera.

So I would just read the manuals on that stuff. When something new came out, I had to read about it before I'd even put my fingers on it. I used to print the manual out and go to town on it. What I did is, I finished that manual. I went back to him and showed him the calibration procedure for the studio's deck. What was kind of cool is that, in typical old–school fashion, he's like, "That's OK."

I'm like, "That took all freaking summer to learn how to do this, and 'that's OK' is your response?" He's like, "Yeah, it's all right.

It'll do." When you look up to somebody you admire and they shoot you down immediately, depending on your character you're either going to run away and tuck tail, or you're going to be like, "All right, now I'm going to get you back." So, what happened was, he was teaching me to be competitive.

Sometimes your best isn't good enough. I carry that with me to this day. Even though you think you may be doing the best you can, there may still be an opportunity for you to do better than that. It encourages me to this day to keep pushing myself, to keep exploring new opportunities and options for myself, to grow. I'm 40 years old. I turned 40 in May. I still have this thing where I can never stop learning about being a record producer or being a recording engineer.

I still feel like there's more for me to learn, to the point where I'd be willing to intern for somebody even at 40 years old. I know that sounds really silly to some people. But if you're 40 years old and you're like me, no matter how good you might think you are, there are people that are still better at it than you. They might even be younger than you. So I'm always, always asking questions.

I am completely a product of the mentorship and support I've received over the years, either in the recording industry from the people that I've worked for and worked with, or in the tech industry. I used to call Tom Reichenbach—God rest his soul—I used to call Tom Reichenbach at Cinemag and sit on the phone with him for hours and talk with him about transformers. Oliver Archut—God rest his soul—same way. I just used to find people that knew more than me, and just pour myself a cup of coffee, and they were willing to share what they knew. That was the difference.

Now I'm that person, even though I feel like I'm not ready to be that person. But at the time, I was just like the little kid just lapping it up. "Oh the hysteresis happens like this, and if you shift these values around, kiddo, this is what happens. And haha." And I'm just sitting there writing it down, like this is good stuff. And that built the lexicon and the dictionary that's in my head. That encyclopedia that spins around in a circle constantly whenever I look at equipment and where people feel equipment fails them.

All of those things formed who I am, and it's the same way with Gabriel. His mentorship, his ability to push me, to know how to push me, to see things in myself that I didn't see in myself—they all influenced me in a million and one ways. And I know this is going to sound really funny, but all I've really tried to do with Zulu is get back to when I was 16—when I was 16 years old and I started in this, and all I really wanted to do was know how to rap. I didn't want to be an engineer. I didn't want to make beats. I just wanted to rhyme. And yet, that studio had that sound, man. And so I've done everything that I can to develop this device to basically be like that time machine to take me back to 1993 because that was like... that was a magic time for people my age. And after a while, there was no more tape. But I got to live with it in a way that most people didn't.

I mean, a 16-year-old kid my age that didn't get that experience, ten years later, near 26, people were phasing tape out. I don't even know if they were still making Ampex 456 in 2003, but that would have been the age that young man might have got out of college and got into studios and started to really learn how to do stuff. That was when everybody's transitioning away completely. They'd already done the ADAT shift into digital recording with computers, so if you missed that boat then that frame of reference was completely missed by you. Completely. You just didn't know. I meet people that are older than me that started making music later than I did on the timeline, and they have no experience with what tape sounded like on drums, or vocals, or any of that stuff. They're clueless.

Where you're from does affect where you go when it comes to stuff like art, right? SSL did a demo here in my town and they had the "Thriller" multitracks in the truck, right? The song "Thriller," by Michael Jackson?

Matt: Yeah.

Langston: And they were obviously some kind of transfer from tape to digital. And the thing that was amazing to all these young engineers, guys who were fresh out of broadcast school and all of that, was the complete and absolute lack of all those things that you hear when you record yourself at home or even in a modern studio. They were just like, "Dude, there's nothing above 12k. There's no 8k on these lead vocals, and yet everything fits together so perfectly." And I said, "There's a lot more to it than what I'm gonna say, but this would not have sounded like this without tape." There's an arcane lack of detail in those multitracks that is gorgeous that just makes so much sense across the entire broadband. And I know what that sounds like 'cause I've heard it over and over again.

I know what it's like to put a 414 to tape on a female's voice and to expect something back. I mean a 414 isn't that fun to listen to in the first place, but you know what it's gonna do on a woman. And then you add in the component of maybe some decent clean gain staging, and then you throw in analog tape, and forget it. What you're managing at that point is the performance, you're not managing the audio. It's like what Gabriel taught me about competitiveness, and being studious, and being learned so that when you go into a situation you always have your brain focused on solving things and fixing things and addressing things as they happen at the speed of sound. All those things frame how

I look at the process of recording, but especially when I apply that experience to the process of developing equipment for recording.

## The Beginner's Mind

Matt: You've touched on something I mention on the show periodically, and that is the concept of the beginner's mind. You said that even at 40, you'd be willing to go and intern for someone, just to keep learning. I agree completely. I'm 47 now, and I'm getting ready to go in September to Mix with the Masters with Tchad Blake.

Langston: Congratulations.

Matt: Thank you, thank you. A few of my friends were like, "Why are you gonna go to that? That seems like something for beginners." And I'm like, "Are you kidding? No. That's not what it is at all."

Langston: Why is it that when it comes to recording and engineering, there's a limit to how long it takes you to get good, right? There's a point where you're just good. And yet, when you're a musician, there's never a point you stop learning. There's musicians that go to clinics—like if Neil Peart gave a clinic right now, people would go. And they might be older than him, OK? They might be jazz drummers that just want to learn, or they want to hang with him. They want to absorb some of his energy.

Why are we so withdrawn from the fact that we work on music? We're not professor emeritus of economics or something like that, where it's abstract and complete, and it's mathematical and predictable. This is art. So anything that you can do to get better at art, no matter what age you are—I mean, nobody can gauge when somebody's maturity is supposed to be somewhere with the skill set, right?

I'm an educator as well as a person that works on music. I've taught many people how to do this. And everybody's maturity and everybody's willingness and readiness to learn something is different. There is no such thing as the same singular timeline for every student. Like by the time you're 12, you should know how to do this with a microphone. There's people that don't even know how to hold a mic that are 40 years old, 50 years old, and they've seen people do it on television, and they still don't know what to do with it. They still don't know where to speak into it. And as a person that teaches, you have to be ready to know that some people will come to you lacking things. And as a student, you have to be honest with yourself, and say, "I lack this. I lack the ability to hear *this* that these guys talk about," or, "I lack the ability to know what's art and what's pastiche."

And sometimes, having a person there that's experienced, whether it's with music or the technical side of an art, is the best cheat code you can ever enter into your life, man. So yeah, I mean, your friends can say that, but it's not like you can just get Tchad Blake on YouTube on his channel, and pick his brain, and he's gonna spill his beans to you. You gotta be there with the man, and he's gotta see you throw down. Just like karate and kung fu, you can't just go on YouTube and become a ninja. You have to walk across the fire, man. That's the beauty of art. Unless you want this shit, you're not gonna get it. And that's what I loved about it. Unless you wanted it, and you proved your want and your desire, you were never gonna have those things. No one was gonna share those secrets with you because you didn't prove yourself. And you're doing that.

Matt: I'll give you another example. I've been friends with Andrew Scheps for some time and instantly really connected with him. I saw him recently at a conference, and I said, "Oh, I see you just did Mix with the Masters. How was it?" He said, "Oh man, it was great." And he told me all about it. And I said, "While I'd love to see you do it, Andrew, I really would love to see Tchad Blake." He goes, "Oh, you don't want to see my thing." He said, "But Tchad Blake, oh my God. I'd want to see that myself."

When I hear somebody like Andrew Scheps say that—and he's very popular right now—that just validates it for me. He doesn't think he's the smartest person in the room. You know, I bet I could spend a week with you and you could teach me so much about the tech end of it, the building part of it, and many other aspects of it. And vice versa. You could probably spend a week with me, and there's so much that we could learn from each other.

Langston: Yes.

Matt: So just to kind of hit it with a hammer and nail it all the way in: There's always more time and always more people to learn from, no matter what you think you know.

Langston: Right. Yeah, I mean, I watched some footage of Joel Hamilton with Universal Audio at his place at Studio G. Joel is a user of Zulu, an endorser of it. And right after we had visited him, he had done this session with Universal Audio with Fabrice Dupont where they recorded, and then they mixed, and they used all this gear and everything else. And Joel went over these different miking techniques, and for the drums. And some of the stuff was like, "Wow, that's different." And some of the stuff was like, "I thought I was the only one that did that." And one of the things that popped into my head is that sometimes these opportunities for us to go and learn from other people, to visit with them, to speak with them, is also a way for you to know what clan you belong to in the art world.

There are people that are abstract artists, and there are people that are classic artists in the classic sense. They draw faces, and bodies, and hands, and feet, and fruit. And then there's people like Basquiat that deform forms. And their artwork is just as beautiful, and sometimes ten times more striking and eye-catching than a classic artist, right? And so sometimes you gotta know like, Hey man, I'm more like in the Basquiat or Pollock world than I am in the Rembrandt world of painting or even at the level of Van Gogh. I really don't like forms, I like stuff, or I like three–dimensional art. And the same thing is true with audio. Sometimes you just have to know whose philosophies fits you better.

If you're trying to record squirrels catching nuts at the bottom of a tree, then it kind of doesn't make sense all the time to go and try to become the best drum recorder, when you should really focus on nature and the techniques that they adopt. Or if you're trying to get better at electric guitars, well find the guy that's great at that. Or if you just like doing weird, wacky stuff in the studio then get with Eric Valentine, or Joel Hamilton, or any of these other great record producers that bend the rules to their whim. Right? They're like air benders. They're magicians of a sort. And just accept that that's your thing.

There's far too many people trying to do everything with their career. I'm not saying I'm incapable of recording a symphony orchestra, but I like bands. And I like heavy, over-the-top bands, and hip-hop music, and big drums, and mean guitars, and pop music with an attitude. That's my thing. That's my flavor. And I kind of want to learn from the people that do that more than I just want to pick up information from anywhere that still may or may not get me closer to my goal. Like Tchad Blake is a bad dude. And he's all about the tone, all about the artifact, all about the overshoot, right?—and how to manipulate that into impact.

And if that's your style, why wouldn't you learn from him? That makes more sense to me than going some other direction totally. So I totally get what Andrew Scheps is saying. Because when you listen to the stuff these guys do, it's amazing, and if you had an opportunity to learn from it, I'd be right in line with you, man.

Matt: Yeah, it's funny. When I think of Zulu as a product, I think, "Man, that's something Tchad Blake would be using."

Langston: Well tell him that when you see him.

Matt: I'll tell him that.

Langston: The thing about Zulu is that it gives you the chance to revisit the entire premise of how you also record music. We live in a mixing–heavy world, and I think what's kind of bizarre to me, as a guy that started out with the musicians from day one, I never got introduced to audio as a static, the-party's-over kind of thing. We live in a world now where people don't even interact with the musicians, right?

Matt: Yeah.

Langston: They have no relationship with them. They have no connection to them. They simply are an email address, a financial instrument, and some files. That's their world, right? And there's nothing wrong with that, but there is something to be said about being there when the band first comes in, helping them load their stuff in, hearing them rehearse, giving them any information that they may need, making sure that they're comfortable, connecting with them, spending that time. People are always in a hurry to record people. People are always in a hurry to get rid of people, and I used to spend time with people. When I worked in Philadelphia, man, we'd hang before the session. The guys would be like, "Yeah, that joint last night..."

And you listen to the players talk and kibitz around and all that, and you connect with people, and you begin to learn them. And you begin to kind of bond and merge yourself into their energy. And that's missing on so many levels now.

And the same approach is true with audio. When you record, it's more like you're just trying to survive the process rather than it being something enjoyable for you. And I want people to remember that audio isn't something you have to worry about, it's something you work with. There's a difference. And a lot of the operating principles now are about being safe. It used to be a world where, if you were in the red, well does it sound good? Now it's like, well if you go past this point, you screwed up. That's it, you ruined it.

Matt: Yep.

Langston: And that's hard for me to address when... I mean, unless you make some egregious error in a lot of other realms, that's not true. I mean, if you happen to make the line a little bit fatter on a painting than you intended to, you might still be able to fix that, or fake it and make that error look like it was intentional. Versus with the way technology is right now, you just screw up and that's it. It's almost worse than whatever penalty you incurred with tape. I mean, yeah, if you messed up on tape, and you bummed the whole take, that's fine. But just to say you recorded it too hot, there might still be a way to save it. I mean, I read an article not too long ago that Janet Jackson's *Control* was cut something crazy, like +12.

Matt: Really?

Langston: Yeah, man. The whole LP. And you know why? It's because they calibrated the deck wrong. They thought they were hitting at +6 or +9, and it was really +12, OK? And what was impressed upon me is that, if you could screw up that bad and make some platinum, classic, seminal example of the pop sound that was Janet Jackson's coming out party—and Jimmy Jam and Terry Lewis learned this technique, not the +12 part, but the record the tape hot part from Prince. When they were with Prince, they had learned that distortion gives things definition. Especially to tape.

So they were just trying to do the same thing with the drum machines, and the synthesizers, and the synth basses, and all of that stuff. They really didn't have any live instrumentation on that album. Not in the traditional sense. I mean, they were playing this stuff, but they didn't really have players on stringed instruments or drums. It was mostly synthetic. And they were just trying to give this stuff some soul, some attitude, some character. And what happened is, I believe the machine was calibrated incorrectly, so that when they were hitting +6 on the machine, they were really hitting +12.

And yet, if you go back and you listen to *Control*, it's glorious. I mean, go and try to take a LinnDrum right now with a copy of any DAW, and try to make it sound like that. It's one of those things where you just gotta have it the right way, and they even had to hire a special mix engineer to deal with the really hot levels, but the sound was glorious.

And I really feel like when you add that component back into the recording process where even the recording medium, even the equipment, has a mind and a soul of its own that's gonna forever be imprinted on your audio, and you can actually expect it to react to you, the human input—that changes the way you approach music. So for me, as an engineer, that's how I was raised in it. That was part of the process—the gear was gonna talk to you. It was either gonna sound bad, or it was gonna sound great, but there was a bigger margin of great yet inappropriate. There was the naughty side of it.

## Philosophy, Family, and Running a Business

Matt: Where did you go to school?

Langston: I went to Le Moyne College.

Matt: And what did you study?

Langston: Philosophy.

Matt: Philosophy, no shit?

Langston: Right. I did computer science, as well, as a concentration. But really it was philosophy with a concentration in informal logic.

Matt: Are there any quotes that you live by that drive you?

Langston: Well, I had a professor at Le Moyne College who was a bit of a prodigy. His name was James Lacey, Dr. James Lacey. And he was, I think, under 40, and he'd already been published by Cambridge. This guy was crazy intelligent. Kind of like crazy, off the chain, brilliant guy, right? Dr. Leahy says one day—we're talking about Plato and Socrates—and he says, "The minute you become a philosopher, you've signed your own death sentence." What he meant by that was when you reject what society tells you, society's going to try to kill you. Not necessarily physically, even though sometimes that happened, like they had to make Socrates drink hemlock, but your soul, your spirit, your image, your reputation, the way you feel about people, the way people feel about you, society will try to destroy that about you.

My reaction to that was atypical. I just like, "Ah, that's kinda cool." This fake me, that the world tells me I need to be, right, this imaginary person that I've been raised to be—you can only be *this* when you grow up, or *you're never going to be that guy,* or *only these people are ever in charge of this,* or *only these people ever invent stuff.* I shed that in that moment in college. I rejected that crap that I was going to be limited by what people told me I could and couldn't do. I think it's a full circle thing for me to remember that quote. I'm glad you asked me that. I'm glad that I became the person that I am rather than what society told me to be.

Here's a case in point. My family came to America in 1913 on my mother's side. My grandmother, who was the daughter of my great–grandmother who came to America, was a tube engineer at General Electric during the civil rights movement and was not ever considered brilliant in her own right, was not ever considered smart, and yet she taught other people how to build tube equipment, and she had no college education, no formal training. She was just a brilliant, brilliant woman and was not going to be allowed to ever supervise other people by one of the more known names in society, General Electric.

We'd be like, "Oh, they're great. They make technology and stuff." Yeah, but they were a product of their time. Segregation was real even then, along with racism, which it still is now, but especially sexism. A woman was never going to be as smart as a man. Growing up, I faced the same forces that my grandmother faced at General Electric, like, "Well, *these* people go to NASA, and *these* people are scientists, and *these* people are technicians." Yet, here I am. I say this in disbelief at times. I don't say this in a conceited manner. Yet here I am, the offspring of the offspring of this woman who used to build tube amps for General Electric.

I run my own company. I talk to other people that run their own companies and develop their own technologies and innovate. If I had listened to what people told me—if I wasn't willing to accept the death of my former self—I would not be the person before you. It's something that just continues to dovetail and spread for me, man. Like when I walked into that truck from SSL, they're like, "Oh, we know about Zulu." It's like, "SSL knows about Zulu?" We're not that big of a company. Our name, our brand, is not that mature. We just released Zulu in February of this year, and yet companies like that, other peers and competitors, are well aware of this product.

It's very interesting to be in the position that I'm in as an inventor, but also as a businessperson, and to reflect on these things that have been taught to me in reference to not only my education but my upbringing and my ancestry. That is probably the quote I carry with me all the time. If you're ready to be a philosopher, if you're ready to look at the way things work and not be afraid to jump outside the box, then you have to be willing to let your former self die and take on the new identity that you choose for yourself.

Matt: Are there any routines that you do on a daily basis, that get you set for your day? I always bring up the examples of some people like to go running, some people smoke pot, some people meditate.

Langston: My thing that keeps me sane is I pray. I have two small daughters, thirteen and nine, Nayela and Aaliyah. I didn't grow up in the most religious household. My mother was Roman Catholic, for whatever that's worth, but I have found my way through life. Prayer has been one of the places that grounds me and keeps me focused in terms of, none of this belongs to me, right? When you realize that whatever you have in your hands—at least in that sense, the religious Christian sense—that whatever you possess is really meant to be given away. For me, it's not like I need to acquire anything today.

That's what every day is like for me. I don't need to go conquer the world or have this in my hand to know that I did something. For me, it's like, Who am I going to help today? Who am I going to bless today? Who am I going to be kind to? Who is my invention going to make happy, right? It encourages me to make new designs. It encourages me to perfect designs. It encourages me to revisit the way I work, how efficiently my business works, how I deal with other people so that I continue to be that person rather than somebody that looks at the dollars and cents of things and says, "Well, I need to make $20,000 this month."

*"I don't need to go conquer the world or have this in my hand to know that I did something. For me, it's like, Who am I going to help today? Who am I going to bless today? Who am I going to be kind to?"*

It's like none of this belongs to me. I only hold it for an instant, then it's out of my hand. Now, I might have money, food, the love of people, material possessions along the way, but if you hold onto that, at least in my sense, then you're losing sight of what's important. I would not be able to do what I do if I had not disconnected myself from the acquisition of things. To be an inventor, not the most effective pickup line in the world, if you get my drift. To be able to disconnect yourself from, "If I don't do this then I don't get this," rather than, "This is my vision, and I just want to see the end of this process." I want to see this come to life. That is more important to me, and that is what drives me more so than the aftereffects of that invention or the aftereffects of helping others or the aftereffects of when I sell this many or get these people to endorse the product, if this company signs on or that business is interested in us. Those sorts of things matter to me as a businessperson, but as a human being, they don't matter to me in the same way. I think that if anything, they're the side effect of what giving it away means to me, because I didn't have to turn this into something I sell to people.

I could've just given it to myself. I could've kept it. I could've been like, "No, I'm not sharing that with anybody." Because I had decided to turn it into something that became the world's, effectively—Zulus are all over the planet now—it widened my vision and widened my scope, and it also helped me to realize new things that I could be doing with my gifts and talents with this company and beyond. To go back to my simple, plain-Jane answer: I wake up every morning, and I pray. That's how I know how my day has officially started is when I end that.

Matt: You said that being an inventor is a major part of your life really, but what are the other things that you do daily that comprise your world?

Langston: The main thing that I do besides Handsome Audio is I work as a record producer. People come to me with their projects and ask me to turn them into albums. I also work on my own stuff, perform it, record it. Between that and Handsome Audio it's a lot, plus I'm a parent. That ties up my time quite a bit. My day typically is checking in on my projects, making sure that they're progressing, making sure that my timetable is being met, making sure that things are being done to the right accord.

A lot of the projects that I deal with involve session musicians. I don't necessarily just deal with "the band" by itself anymore. I typically am asked to hire out for projects. I deal with many different people just for the sake of one song. When I find some free moments, typically I will check in at the factories that manufacture the different components and assemblies that go into making Zulu. I check in on the different entities and see where they're at, make sure that the box house is happy, make sure that cable assemblies are being done right or the circuit boards are coming in the door or the subassemblies from the electronics house are coming out OK and where their scheduling is at.

When that's not happening, I'm back in the studio, or I'm planning on the next day. I have a thing where usually what I try to do is a six-hour workday when it comes to the stuff like Handsome Audio. I do about five to six hours of work total in a day, and then I'm done. What I'm doing in that second half of the day is I'm planning the next day. That's how I help myself stay organized. It's a very small business with a lot of responsibility. The same thing is true as a record producer. You're in the studio. There's long hours. There's a lot of turnover and constant deadlines that are coming up, but I try not to overwork myself there either because I'm very sensitive to work effectiveness.

The longer you work at something in a period of time, it can diminish the output, versus if you simply do things in concentrated bursts. If you give yourself a beginning and an end time, and then you rest, you can do some pretty good things, especially when you get older. When you're 40, you're not 18 anymore. You can't stay up for 13, 14 hours straight and expect everything to be gold. You'll miss stuff. I try to avoid being in situations like that quite frequently, to be honest with you.

My days are actually pretty busy with music industry stuff on the independent level, which is where I'm at, and then the music industry stuff with the tech world. That's pretty much a full day for Handsome Audio and Narrative Audio, my studio and production company, but as well, if it's not those things, it's my daughters or personal time. I try to make sure that there's time for that. I try not to make my entire life just work, work, work, work, work.

Matt: Oh man.

Langston: You have to breathe.

Matt: I know that. I got so much grief from my nine-year-old. We were on vacation in New Mexico. I said, "OK, I'm off. I'm going to go to this studio, so hang out with grandma and grandpa." My nine-year-old said, "Dad, tomorrow, no more working. We're on vacation. Stop going to studios."

Langston: Yeah, my daughters will take my phone. The world could be on fire. They don't care, they're taking my phone.

Matt: That's their time.

Langston: I'm glad that they do that because it is hard for me to put it down. It will pull you away from anything that's in front of you. It's amazing that I'll be sitting at a table with a guy with all sorts of credits to his name, and he's fighting the same demons with his phone that I am. I'm just like, "OK, I thought I had a problem too, but...." The thing makes noise, and you just have to look at it. It's like a Ray Bradbury short story. It's like you're attracted to the buzz. You have to flip it over, and when you flip it over, it lights up. Then you get pulled into the magic portal of text messages.

I just leave it in the middle of the table half the time if I can or people will take it from me. I'm good with that. I'm like, "Take my phone. Hide my phone." It is important to have that time with your family and the people that love you. You've got to put that time aside for them, otherwise you can't be effective because that part of you that needs that won't be satisfied, in my opinion. That comes out in your work.

Matt: It always makes me think of Martin Sheen in the opening scenes of *Apocalypse Now* where he says, "When I was home, I wanted to be back in the jungle, and when I was back in the jungle, I wanted to be home." It's like that for me in audio. I don't know if you experience the same thing. When you're in it, you're like, "Oh I'm here, this is great, but I do need to get home at some point." Then once you're home, you're like, "Oh, I gotta get back in the jungle."

Langston: It's amazing to note that there are often times in my career that were so engrossing that the last thing on my mind was home. There used to be a point in my career where it was like that, where when I was in the studio, the musicians were just so good, the material was so phenomenal, that home, food, the bathroom, anything—you, just you didn't care about it because you were in your element. That was a maturity thing. I've learned that as a producer and as a professional and a practitioner, a master practitioner if you will, you have to begin to insert into the relationships you build with people a certain degree of respect for your personal life that has no financial value, meaning that no matter how much people pay me, I'm not sacrificing the time I have with my children.

If they really want me and they really want to work with me and experience my gifts and talents, they have to accept that. There are people that are so worried about losing money and losing clients that they will never take that stand, but the thing about little kids and your family and your spouse, your loved one, your girlfriend, your wife, whoever is important to you in your life, right, you don't get that time back. No matter if you make $30,000 doing a band's LP, that can't buy that time back. You don't get to repurchase your baby's first steps or that assembly that your daughter plays cello at. You don't get that time back.

If you don't stand up for that, then no one's going to stand up for it for you. You have to be able to assert that to your clients, like, "Look, this is important to me. This is the time that I need for my family, and we're going to have to reconvene at this time." If you at least follow the path that I'm on, if people give you crap about that, tell them, "Look, I can't budge." If they're going to walk, show them the door. Be kind about it, be professional, but at the same time, if they're going to sit there and treat you like that over your family, I can guarantee that won't be the last time you butt heads with them about stuff like that. It'll keep coming up.

There'll be other things that are going to manifest in that relationship that will impact you professionally that you'll regret. It's a simple rule I have: family first. I don't lose clients like that, but I also don't get clients that disrespect me either. I don't get people that come in here and disrespect the time that I have with my family. I have clients that tell me, "You know what? We've done this many hours. We want to make sure you have time with your kids." That's something I worked hard to get, but I got it now. That's important to—I think—most people that have children, and it can happen for you if you make that your thing. It can.

I see guys that have the best credits in the world, and they'll still spend time with their kids. They still will make that time. If they can do it, and they got Grammys and platinum records and money, then cover band X is not going to interrupt my time or whatever. If important people can do it, then people that are not as important as those important people can do it too. We can do it as novices as well as people at the top of the chart.

Matt: On that note, I'm going to go and join my two little guys in my life to make dinner.

Langston: The munchkins, I love it.

Matt: Yeah. I really enjoyed listening to what you had to say. I appreciate you taking the time to speak with me. Thanks again. Give me a couple websites where people can find out more about you.

Langston: The most important website that you can visit is going to be handsomeaudio.com, which is the home page of Zulu, the world's first passive analog tape simulator. There you will at least find the information about the design and the device and all the wonderful things that make Zulu, Zulu. As well, if you are a member of gearslutz.com, there are quite a few threads on there about Zulu that are worth reading. There are also a lot of hints and tips that are exchanged on there. In addition, if you have a Facebook account, there is a group on there that you can join by invite or by request called Handsome Audio Analog Renaissance, which is the power users' forum for Zulu, which is where a lot of Grammy–winning and platinum engineers frequent and share tips on how they use Zulu.

Just those couple of different resources right there will really fill you in about some of my philosophies and also about this wonderful little box of joy, that's going to become a big box of joy soon, to help you figure out if it's for you or not. That would be where you'd really get your start as far as understanding why I've started this conversation about analog tape and how we can reintegrate the soul and tonality of it into the recording and mixing process in 2017 and beyond.

Matt: Once again, thanks for taking the time to chat with me. It's been a pleasure.

Langston: Oh anytime, my man. Thank you for the opportunity.

Take care, man. Have a good one.

# Mark Kilborn

## Backstory and Introduction

Mark Kilborn is a sound designer, mixer, and implementer with over a decade of experience in sound for video games. He has worked on various game franchises, including Borderlands, Forza Motorsport, Brothers in Arms, Tony Hawk, and Project Gotham Racing. For the last eight years he has served as one of the audio directors for the Call of Duty series, collaborating with teams of sound designers around the world on various projects, including Modern Warfare 3, Advanced Warfare, Black Ops 1-3, Exo Zombies, Call of Duty Online, and Modern Warfare Remastered. After Mark and his wife had twins in 2015, he stepped down from the audio director role and worked as a principal audio designer from his home studio. In 2018, he returned to his previous role.

Mark first made contact with me in January of 2016. I could tell right away that he was a serious audio pro from his work on Call of Duty and other titles. But his writing also revealed that he was just a good person and a family man.

Mark and I stayed in touch and he became, as I like to think of him in the TV drama sense, my Confidential Informant into the world of game sound. I could run names past him and vet people to come on the show. In February of 2017, I finally met Mark in person when he came to San Francisco for the Game Developers Conference. We set up at a coffee shop, and amongst the noise of patron's orders being called out and coffee beans being ground, we conducted an interview.

Since then Mark has stayed a steadfast supporter of the podcast. He always has a lead on a person to interview and words off encouragement about the latest show. Mark is just one of those people who has become a part of my ecosystem. His messages are like the sounds of birds in the forest—when I read them, I know that all is well in my podcast world because Mark is chiming in to comment on what he got out of an episode.

It's messages like these that keep me going because I know my efforts are making a difference.

Mark lives in Madison, Wisconsin, with his wife, three kids, two dogs, and too much snow.

Enjoy the interview!

-Matt

# Interview with Mark Kilborn

Matt: Welcome to the podcast.

Mark: Thank you for having me.

Matt: This is the first time I've done an interview in a coffee shop, much less a Starbucks, but here we are. As I always say, coffee is the thing that brings people together and gets people to open up. Of course, you're having a tea, but that still counts. Is there caffeine in there?

Mark: Yes, there is.

## Life at Activision

Matt: OK. So we're in downtown San Francisco and you're here in town for the Game Developer's Conference. Tell me a little bit about your background, as far as gaming and audio is concerned, and why you come to the Developer's Conference.

Mark: I decided I wanted to do this when I was a little kid. Went to school at Full Sail around early 2000s, I graduated 2004. First job was at a post-production studio in Detroit, strangely enough. I moved there briefly after school; then I came back to Texas, which is where I had lived prior.

I had discovered that a friend, who was in a band I had been playing shows with when I was younger, was doing sound for games. I told him what I was trying to achieve, that I wanted to get into game sound professionally. Eventually, he called me one day and said, "Hey, I need an extra pair of hands on this Tony Hawk game. Do you want to help me out?" So I instantly quit my job at a post studio and went to work with him, so that's how I got into games.

I came to the Game Developer's Conference in 2006 for the first time. Outside of E3, it's the biggest trade show for the industry. But it's really aimed at the developers rather than the press. Whereas E3 is showing off new games to press and fans, GDC is aimed at developers, so we get to see new tools and technologies. We get to go to talks and learn from each other.

I think last year, they had around 70,000 people in town for this. It's a pretty tremendous event. Then, there's a ton of audio people here, as well. So we spend the week drinking, and hanging out, and talking about stuff. It's a lot of fun and it's educational.

Matt: Do you work for a particular company?

Mark: Yes, I work for Activision.

Matt: What is your job there?

Mark: My title now is Audio Principal. Until late last year, I was an audio director. I kind of shifted roles because I wanted to spend more time with my kids, frankly.

I work on the *Call of Duty* series. I've worked on almost every game since "Black Ops 1," in varying capacities. On some games I assisted with certain sections of the game, on others I was

*"The zombies campaign for 'Advanced Warfare' in 2014 was something I did."*

directing certain pieces of audio for it. The zombies campaign for "Advanced Warfare" in 2014 was something I did. I was the audio director for the "Modern Warfare Remastered" game that came out late last year. Then, in other games, I was directing a small team that was contributing to a section of the game. But now, as an audio principle, I'm basically back to being a sound engineer. Although, they sometimes give me ownership of smaller sections of things. I'm working on a section for an upcoming game with one guy working with me.

But it's nice. It's less responsibility, and I work from home now. I got to move home. I have one-year-old twins, so it's nice to be able to be in my studio at home. If my wife needs help for 30 minutes, I can run downstairs and help out, then get back to work. So it's a really nice set up.

Matt: I'm curious how the day–to–day works for you. Tell me more about the functionality of it all for you.

Mark: It's definitely different compared to doing post production or music, in terms of day–to–day flow—at least compared to post; I haven't done music work professionally; I've only done it as being in a band. But compared to doing post production professionally, we would have projects that would come in that would be over in a day or two.

Now, I'm on a project for 12 months, maybe longer. So we tend to break up our work into sprints of like a month or two. We're trying to complete small sections of the game. We may not even be completing them; we may be just trying to get them up to a certain level of quality. Then we'll go work on another section of the game, then we'll come back and push things further.

So it's a little strange. You don't get that sense of quick accomplishment that you get with smaller projects. It can actually become a bit of a slog when you're six months from shipping and you feel like you haven't actually completed anything in half a year.

But in terms of what I do day–to–day, it's a lot of different things; it really depends on where the area that I'm responsible

*"I have days where I make sounds all day in my DAW. I have days where I'm outside recording sound effects. I have days where I am scripting. ...I'll spend two days or three days just hooking sounds up in the game engine."*

for is, at any given point. I have days where I sit there and make sounds all day in my DAW. I have days where I'm outside recording sound effects. I have days where I am scripting. We have a scripting language for our engine that's very similar to C, the programming language, and I'll spend two days or three days just hooking sounds up in the game engine.

Matt: The engine inside a game that processes it all within a gaming console, I don't understand how that works. I don't understand how you take all of these different components and toss them into this "engine." Can you decipher that for those of us who are more musically inclined?

Mark: Sure. I've tried to explain this for years. I stumbled upon a perfect analogy one day with another engineer I know who does music stuff. This is simplifying it a bit, but the best way I've found to explain it is, imagine you have a giant sampler, like Kontakt. It's hard for me to even say how much RAM we have, now that we've moved to the PlayStation 4 and the Xbox One. We're not thinking about RAM anymore because the consoles have eight gigs.

But imagine you've got a gig of RAM, maybe a little bit more. What you do is, you make a bunch of sounds and you load them into this sampler. Then you teach the game when to play each of the individual sounds out of the sampler. When it plays them, it can pitch them up and down, it can modulate the volume, it can do a lot of different things.

Then it plays those samples into a 64-channel mixer, which we have as part of our game engine. Each channel has EQ filtering and volume control. Then, those sounds get routed through busses and then they go on a master. So effectively what we're doing is, we're loading a bunch of sounds into a sampler. We're telling the game, these are the circumstances in which you play them, and this is what you do with the mixer when you play them so that it will pan them correctly in surround. It'll also move the faders up and down.

It's all based on data that's coming from the game. When the game is playing, the audio engine is getting this huge spew of data from the game. Like, here's where the player is in the 3D world and then, this door just slammed shut. Here's where that is. It'll look and say, hey, the distance to that sound is X, so based on that, I'm gonna pull the fader down this much. Hey, there's a wall in between it, so I'm gonna apply this low pass filter to it. We're kind of teaching a game how to mix itself and how to trigger all of the sounds as it plays. Does that make a little more sense?

Matt: It does make a lot of sense. Camden Stoddard was on the show as a guest in a previous episode, so we got a little taste of that from him. What I'm starting to understand is that beyond getting all the audio pieces together, there's actually an art to implementing those sounds within these engines.

Mark: Yeah, absolutely. The way you implement determines how the sound is mixed when it's played back, so there's a huge creative piece there. Especially in *Call of Duty*, for example, we have players firing guns constantly because it's a shooting game. If we put one single gunshot on a player's gun, they're gonna hear the same shot over and over again. So we break them up into multiple different layers.

There's the transient, there's the body of the shot, there's the tail, there's the mechanical sound of the gun moving. There may be a shell ejection sound, or a shell hitting the surface material below them, which changes based on what they're standing on. So we have to create all these elements, and put them all in together, that all get triggered every time the shot gets fired. Then, for each one of those elements, there would be ten variations.

Those are the two areas where the implementation really comes into play, at least with sound effects. Music is another thing entirely. But you have to create these little pools of sound that can be dynamically stacked together and played—and that sound interesting and different every time the player fires them, or triggers them, or whatever the sound is. A can falling off of a table is the same thing.

Matt: So what about the pressure of getting the job done, versus putting the quality into it? I mean, if there was ever an audio profession that exemplified the term minutia, this would be it, in my opinion.

Mark: Absolutely.

Matt: So how do you manage the pressure? I know that you have these milestones that you have to meet, so how does that come into play?

Mark: It's tough, man. Sometimes, it is really tough. We work a lot of long hours sometimes. I live in Microsoft Excel; I have everything plotted out in a spreadsheet. I know every gun in the game. I know every layer of every gun. I know every physics object, every random television in a corner that you can blow up.

We have lists of everything. We schedule this stuff out and we build it piece by piece.

One thing that I've found helps us—and here, I'm stealing a term from our art department—is they have this concept called the "beautiful corner." What they do with that is they take a small section of the game and they get that to a finished state of

*"We'll get one or two guns completely done. We'll get a grenade explosion done, we'll get a handful of sounds done, some Foley movement–type sounds done so that we have a clear target of what this game is gonna sound like when it's finished."*

quality. Like if you walked to that one area of that one mission of the game and look at it, it looks done.

So what we'll often do earlier on in the project with audio, is we'll get one or two guns completely done. We'll get a grenade explosion done, we'll get a handful of sounds done, some Foley movement–type sounds done so that we have a clear target of what this game is gonna sound like when it's finished, as long as you're in this one place, firing this one particular gun, doing this one particular thing. Then we use that as our reference point for building the rest of it—in terms of quality, but also in terms of time. We track how long it takes to build that section of the game. Then, we look at the rest of the game and kind of schedule it out. See if we can get it done in the amount of time we have left, which sometimes we can, sometimes we can't. Sometimes we can if we work a little harder, so we put in the extra hours and we get it done.

It also depends on how hard you're willing to push. A lot of us in the COD world are very competitive. We want it to sound great. We just are willing to put a lot of effort in.

Matt: Because these are big titles you're talking about.

Mark: Yes.

Matt: I don't really play all that much, in terms of games. Here and there with my kids. I've mentioned on the show before, *Star Wars Battlefront* is one game I enjoy playing but that's really about it. But I know those other titles because I hear about them all the time.

Mark: Yeah. Each year's game has got a campaign, which is a story mode that's four to seven hours in length. It's got a multiplayer mode that has a dozen or more multiplayer maps where people can run around and shoot each other with various game modes.

Some years, although I guess the last couple of years we've had this, we have a Zombies mode, where you've got new maps with these zombie creatures that you're fighting. Often, those have a story to go along with it. We have people we cast for that. So yeah, they're really big games.

Matt: In terms of the number of people involved in this, just on the audio side, at least at Activision, roughly what would you say?

Mark: It varies by project, but I would say it's generally around 15 to 20 people internally working on sound design and hook up. Then, beyond that we have external studios that handle our voice recording. We have a composer, we have a Talent Management Department that handles casting and contracts. I mean, you can kind of get one or two degrees removed from audio. But internally, we usually have 15 to 20 people working on just sound for the game. Not counting our external people.

Matt: Which, I guess, for the workload that you're describing seems kind of small.

Mark: It sometimes is.

Again, it depends on how complicated we go. In a given year, some of the games are a little more complicated than others, in terms of how we're building assets for them. But yeah, some years it's a little tight. We just pull together and we get through it.

Matt: This is a salary job for you, I take it?

Mark: Yes. A lot of us are salaried. Obviously, the external people we contract are not. They're paid however they're paid, I don't even know, I don't manage that. But yeah, for most of us internal, it's salary.

Matt: And you have health insurance, obviously; it's like a regular day gig.

Mark: Yeah. It's a full time job.

## Getting a Foot in the Game Audio Door

Matt: But it's hard to get into, isn't it?

Mark: It is hard to get into. We're having this problem in the game industry where we're trying to get games done with less resources, but we're trying to hit a bigger scope. What a lot of people don't consider when they look at video games is that the price of a video game has not changed much in the last 20 to 30 years.

When I was eight years old and my dad bought me a Nintendo game, that was 50 bucks, in 1988. Now, today, a video game is 60 dollars. So if you think about it, the price of a video game has increased 10 dollars in 30 years. But we're many console generations past—and the amount of art, the amount of audio, the amount of animation, the requirements have gone through the roof. The scope of these games has gotten massive.

So we're now in a position where we have to get a lot done without growing our budget that much. We have to sell a lot of copies of these games. So that's created a situation where we really need to have very senior experienced people working on the games. In the last, I'd say, five or six years, entry level, lower level opportunities for people to get into game audio and into other fields have been drying up to some degree.

There are still opportunities out there, but it's nowhere near as open as it was 13 or 14 years ago when I got in. Even then, it wasn't as open as it had been in the past. Then, you pair that with the fact there's a lot of schools cranking out audio students, which I'm sure everybody is seeing in all corners of the audio industry. A lot of people want to do game sound, and we're just flooded with entry–level applicants, and there's not a lot of jobs. It's kind of a tough market at the moment. I don't want to be all gloom and doom; there's room for people that are genuinely talented and really willing to work hard. But it is not an easy job to get into.

Matt: Is there any sense of mentorship or bringing people up from the bottom as there was in a large way in the music industry in the past?

Mark: When there were entry–level opportunities at a lot of studios, there was a lot more room for that. Microsoft, for example, still has a big sound department. But they used to have a lot of entry–level opportunities for people to get in. Then, that's where the mentorship would happen, they would grow up through that. They're not doing that as much anymore.

As a result, no, there's not a lot of room for mentorship and, as an industry, we're trying to figure that out. We're kind of going through some experiments now because a lot of people in our field that are more senior level agree that this is a problem. We don't know how to train these young people up.

Forgive me for plugging something, but a group of us just started an organization called the Audio Mentoring Project. The idea is, we have a handful of experts for various game companies that work in audio in fields like voice over, music, and sound design implementation.

*"A group of us just started an organization called the Audio Mentoring Project. The idea is, we have a handful of experts for various game companies that work in audio.... We're taking applications for people to be mentored remotely... and we're basically trying to grow up the next generation of audio people."*

We're taking applications for people to be mentored remotely, over the internet, and we're basically trying to grow up the next generation of audio people because we know they can't get jobs with us, so we're giving them access to us in another way.

So we've got the audio director of DICE who worked on *Battlefront* 1 and 2, he just joined up. I'm in there. Damian Kastbauer, who is an implementation expert. He's beyond an expert; he's like the wise old man in the mountain of game audio implementation. He works at PopCap who have games, like, *Plants vs Zombies.*

Matt: *Plants vs Zombies*, OK. I've played *Plants vs Zombies*.

Mark: Yeah, so we've got a bunch of people like that. We've got Becky Allen from PopCap, as well. We're going through these three- to six-month cycles with these students. We're gonna mentor them and help them develop their skills by basically giving them work to do.

We're saying, here are these unpaid projects you're gonna do for us. They're not gonna ship or anything; we're not making money off of it. You're gonna do this project, we're gonna give you feedback, we're gonna teach you everything we can with the goal of trying to raise up some new talent because there's not a lot of places for them to go to get that experience.

Matt: Tell me the name of the organization again.

Mark: It's called The Audio Mentoring Project, and the website is audiomentoring.com. So yeah, we're hoping this will help the knowledge gap because we see it, and I know you guys see it in music as well, when there aren't a lot of studios for people to go work at and come up in. We're hoping this will be a solution. I don't know if this is the magic solution, but we're hoping it will help.

Matt: It would seem that it is a bottleneck to game sound. Because people move up and you need highly trained people to move back in. So this seems like a good solution to what is a significant problem, I would say.

Mark: Oh, it absolutely is. When we go to hire, we get flooded with applications, and the majority of them are below par, they're below what we need, and everybody is seeing this. I hear this constantly, talking with people at other studios, that yeah, we'll post a job listing, we'll get 200 applicants, and maybe one or two of them will be at the level we would consider hiring, and we want to fix that.

Matt: Is it really key for an applicant to have training in game sound, per se, or can somebody from music or post-production easily step into a job like that and be taught the requirements because of their strength and audio knowledge?

Mark: It depends. It depends on how flexible they are with learning. The implementation piece of it is different. When you're building something for linear media, you're building it to picture. When you're building for us, you have to think about how the sounds are going to be broken down and exported out of your DAW and reassembled in the game engine. There are some studios that have dedicated implementation people, but the majority of us don't.

So we need an audio engineer who can not only fire up Pro Tools or Reaper or whatever, and make all these sounds and export them correctly, but also go into a tool like Wwise, or go into a level editor and start putting sounds in the game and hooking it all up. In terms of raw sound design skill, yes, somebody from linear post or from music could certainly come over and probably do the job. The question is, can they get their head around the implementation piece? I've seen some that can, and I've seen some that can't. If you can't, it makes it a lot more difficult, unless you go to one of those few studios out there where they have people that just are dedicated to hooking sounds up in the game. Some people do that, but a lot of studios don't.

Matt: To me, it strikes an image of an octopus in terms of the audio elements involved in gaming.

Mark: Yeah, and there's a certain jack-of-all-trades element to it. I mean, I'll pop open Maya and edit animation files to attach sounds to animations. You have to be unafraid of getting in and tinkering with things and working with things that are a little outside of your sphere of knowledge, so to speak. I mean, yeah, I code a little bit, I work in level editors, I've opened modeling tools, yet I'm not an expert in those things. I'm not as good as an animator, but I can go in there and hook up some animation sounds and other things.

## Gear Lust and Project Budgets

Matt: I often ask guests about gear lust temptations and the flaws in that—but in your position, you're actually being paid a salary. Do you buy gear to use in your work, or does the company buy you the gear you need?

Mark: That's a tricky question for me. Generally, the company buys us the stuff. However, I have my own home studio that I work out of, so I buy my own stuff for that, because I like the idea that, God forbid, if I ever leave Activision, or they cut me or whatever, I have my own set of microphones, I have my own studio. I can go do whatever I want. If I want to go do freelance work, I can do that. Most of us, I would say, have a home studio and a home rig of some sort. It's just kind of good practice to have that to fall back on and to work on stuff outside of work and just kind of develop your skills, right? But generally speaking, when you're working in-house, the company is buying stuff for you, yeah.

We're all affected by gear lust. I don't think anybody escapes that beast. So it certainly affects us. I mean, every year I'm drooling over new synthesizers and mics and all sorts of stuff. I'm pretty restrained about buying the stuff, but I'm certainly looking at it, just like all of us are.

Matt: But if a need comes up for a game you're working on, I'm sure that opens the gateway to just say, "By all means, I need it for the game."

Mark: Yeah. That's where having somebody with control of the purse strings, who understands audio and is reasonable can say, "Well, do we really need this or not?"

Matt: Are we talking about your wife?

Mark: No, not at all [laughs]. Well, at home, yes. As far as my home studio is concerned, yes. At work, when I was the director of the department, that was my job. Now we've got a new guy who has that job as well, and he also has his head on straight about that. So, usually, in most departments, there's an audio director through whom these purchase requests go, and it's that person's job to say, "Is this reasonable or not?" Yes, with the home studio, I have that discussion of, "Yes, dear." Actually, she gave me a really evil look a couple of weeks ago because I was saying, "You know, I've got this awesome Neumann 5.1 surround setup. I think I want to set it up for Atmos at some point in the future." She was like, "How many more speakers is that? Six more?" She knows enough about it to be like, "It's like speakers in the ceiling? No." That's going to be a fun discussion. I'm going to have to do it at some point, because games are moving towards that, but that's going to be a fun discussion when that happens.

Matt: Yeah. Unlike music, where it's hard to sell records, it's not hard to sell games, is it?

Mark: It is at the smaller–budget end of the scale. People that are making independent games, it's very hard to break through that crowd and sell. At the high–budget end of the spectrum, it's not as hard, although there are a lot of games that still don't break even, but the big guys like *Battlefront* and *Call of Duty* and things like that do. So, it's weird. We've gone through a phase kind of like the film industry has, where the middle ground has kind of fallen out of the industry. So, there's the big, huge-budget games that tend to sell well and mostly make their money back, although some of them fail, and then there's a lot of independent games at the bottom end of the scale, and for them it's a crapshoot. You never know what's going to succeed and what's not.

Matt: I'd say it's probably easier to make a record at a lower budget than it is to make a game at a lower budget.

Mark: Yeah.

Matt: In your opinion, is it on par with doing an independent film?

Mark: I can't say for sure, because I haven't worked on any films. I have a lot of friends that have, and I would say it's similar. An independent film versus an independent game is similar. However, the independent games seem to take a lot longer. It seems like a lot of independent games can take between two to four years to make, versus an independent film. It seems like they crank those out in six to 12 months, usually, at least the ones that I have some awareness of. So, it's a longer development cycle, although part of that is that often, independent developers don't have as many people involved, so you get two or three people that are doing everything, versus on an independent film, you can get more of a crew together. So, I'm sure that's part of it.

## Work/Life Balance

Matt: Let's talk a little bit about family, the work–life balance thing. I'm sure you're not immune to it.

Mark: No.

Matt: I'm sure that when these deadlines approach and it's crunch time, then... I mean, you're being paid a salary, so you're not being paid hourly.

Mark: Nope.

Matt: So, how do you square that off at home?

Mark: Well, that's part of why I work from home now, which I'm very thankful I was able to set up. It's rough, man. It's a rough job to have and have a family. I have one-year-old twins, a six-year-old daughter, and a 23-year-old stepdaughter, who's awesome, but she's out of the house. But it's hard, and I know people at studios on the West Coast, and part of the reason I'm not on the West Coast is cost of living is high, which means they tend to have to live farther from work. I know people who go into work on Monday morning during crunch periods and they don't come home till Friday evening. They sleep at work all week and they go home and see their families on the weekends, and that sucks. The way I handle it is by staying away from the West Coast.

Matt: I forget where you live.

Mark: Madison, Wisconsin.

Matt: OK.

Mark: Yeah, and I'm not from there at all.

Matt: Where are you originally from?

Mark: Texas and California. I was born in Southern California, my parents divorced when I was a baby, and I spent my whole childhood bouncing between Texas and Southern California.

Matt: Where in Texas?

Mark: Dallas area. I even spent half of my school years with my mother, and then switched over at fifth grade. So, I really am kind of from both states. But yeah, I moved up to Madison for this job, and—

Matt: That's good. You have dual citizenship between California and Texas? [laughs]

Mark: Sort of, yeah. Part of the way I deal with it is not living on the West Coast, being in a place where my commute was short, and now, obviously, my commute's non-existent, because I work from home. When I wasn't working at home, I'd go home as often as I could, even when I was still working in the building. I would come almost home every night for dinner, have dinner, put my son to bed, read him a book, go back to the office, work more. Now, it's the same thing. I just come down from the studio at dinner time, help put the kids to bed, go back up at about eight o'clock at night and work until one or two a.m., get up the next morning and do it again.

Matt: Wow. The good thing is you're not sitting in a car for that commute, and you are close if there's an emergency. You are close if your wife needs extra help.

Mark: Yeah, and I mean, don't get me wrong, I would love to come to the West Coast and be closer to other audio people, and I've got a lot of friends out here. I would love to come out here, but I just am not willing to give that up, you know? That's why I haven't done it.

Matt: I don't blame you, man. I mean, I think that cost of living thing is key. I mean, Wisconsin compared to California? There's no competition.

Mark: No, it's nuts. Every time people say, "Hey, you should move out to California. Come work out here," I'm like, "I bought a 3,000 square foot house for $270,000. Can you give me that?" No.

So, I've got a yard for my dogs, and I get to put my kids to bed every night, and it's great.

Matt: But you have to deal with my archenemy, snow.

Mark: Yes, I'm with you. It's my archenemy too, and again, working from home has helped with that. I go up to the office for meetings one day a week. Other than that, I stay in as much as possible in winter.

Matt: Where is the office?

Mark: The office is about five minutes from my house. It's really close.

Matt: Oh wow, OK. Not bad.

Mark: So, yeah, other than that, I work from home and I see the snow out the window and I laugh at everybody that has to drive in it, because I hate the snow.

Matt: Is that hard for communication? Do you rely on video chats?

Mark: Video chat, Skype, IM, phone. I have a desk phone. We have an internet phone, we have a networked phone system. So, I have a desk phone at my desk. People can just call me. So that helps, and then if there's some sort of work emergency, I can get in the car and drive up to the office and I'm there really quickly.

Matt: Or, take your snowmobile out.

Mark: Yeah, yeah, yeah. Hike across the arctic tundra to the office.

Matt: Cross country ski there.

Mark: Yeah. It is rough, the winter thing. I don't like it. And growing up in Texas and California, I'm a little spoiled on food. The food in Wisconsin is pretty terrible. I kind of miss that, and I miss living in a big city. We drive down to Chicago every couple of months and spend a weekend there, and that helps. My sister lives there, so we go down and see her and do stuff down there.

Matt: Well, now you, like the rest of us, spend your days sitting behind a computer, and you're also plagued with some snow, so getting exercise is probably a challenge.

Mark: Yep. I've got a treadmill in the basement in front of a big screen TV. I can get on and walk on the treadmill.

Matt: OK.

Mark: Seriously, yeah. I hate the lack of walking around. I obviously need to lose a bit of weight, so that helps with that. Because yeah, I do get a little stir crazy, and then when the weather's nice, I go out and walk outside. I jokingly take smoke breaks. I don't smoke, but I have to go outside and get some sun and some air every once in a while. Yeah, I hate being stuck in an audio cave. As much as I love my job, I hate being stuck in a windowless room. It drives me nuts. My studio at home now has a window. It's not a perfectly treated room; it's a bedroom with a bunch of absorbers and bass traps and stuff in it. But I put up with it because I've got sunlight. It's wonderful. It's a worthy sacrifice for me.

Matt: Another advantage of working at home is you're not always going out to eat. When I had my studio, not too far from where we're at, here in San Francisco, I remember the opening days of that studio. We used to go out to lunch every day, and that adds up, man.

Mark: Oh yeah, it does. Yeah. I eat downstairs in the kitchen. I do make a point of getting out to lunch once a week with the rest of the audio team. We usually go to this place that has great chicken wings. We go eat chicken and talk about audio crap for an hour or so, and that's great, because I do feel like it's important to have that time with them, but yeah, I try to eat out a hell of a lot less. It's better for the budget, for sure.

Matt: We talked about health, mental health, which can be affected by economic stress, which can be affected by a number of things. It probably really does help for you to be at home. That's a level of stress that you can just go, "Eh, I don't have to worry about that."

Mark: Yeah, it reduces the stress of being in a building with, like I said, no windows and having to go outside and all that stuff. Also, it reduces the work–life balance stress too. My wife, I think, is a lot happier that I'm at home, and even though I'm up in the studio all day, on the rare occasion, happens once every week or two, she'll say, "Hey, I really need help for 20 minutes," and I can run downstairs and help her. It doesn't really disrupt my work at all. I can just make up the 20 minutes after I'm done.

So, yeah, it reduces stress on a lot of fronts. It's a much better setup. I'm really hoping that our industry in general will move more towards this. I think it's good for a lot of people. I don't think everybody necessarily needs to be under the same roof at all times, especially when a lot of these studios are located in super–expensive places. It's harder on everybody. I mean, there are studios I love—Double Fine, where Camden works, is an example. They're in downtown San Francisco. Who can afford to live comfortably, working there? As much as I love that studio and I love their games, that's hard on everybody who works there.

Matt: That has a direct effect on everything associated with the business.

Mark: It absolutely does.

Matt: That overhead is tremendous, I'm sure, for anybody on the West Coast.

Mark: Yeah, and I've certainly noticed with Raven, which is the office where I work in Madison, regardless of whether I'm in the building or at home, I've noticed that there are a lot more people there that have a spouse and children compared to studios out here, where it seems like there's a lot more single people, because it's simply easier to have a family in a place where you can afford to house them.

Matt: Or a life. Do you think that it's harder to have a family if you're in a more stressful environment like that?

Mark: Yeah. Definitely. It's hard to have time for it; it's hard to spend enough time with them.

Matt: Or meeting people?

Mark: Yeah. Yeah, it's even harder on that front. So, yeah, I definitely think it's harder to be a game developer and have a family, or want to start a family if you're living in a place like San Francisco or Southern California. It's easier in Washington, to some degree, because it's a little bit cheaper up there, but I know it's still very expensive. Seattle's a big hub for game development. Austin is still one, to some degree, and it's easier there. Even though Austin itself is crazy expensive, as soon as you get outside of the city, the prices just fall off a cliff and housing gets reasonable. But yeah, I kind of wish more developers would move inland a bit, to places like that, where cost of living is more reasonable. I think it would be easier on everyone.

Matt: How critical is it for you to be close to the office? Could you do this job remotely from another city entirely?

Mark: I could, but I think it's helpful to be nearby because it's hard to replace face-to-face communication, and it's hard to troubleshoot something over the phone. Or, I guess it's not hard to troubleshoot something over the phone, it's easier to troubleshoot something when you and a guy are sitting there looking at a screen together, solving it. So I definitely think there's a value in having access to the building. But I could do it remotely. I think I could, and I know a few people that do. There are a handful of people in various roles within Activision that work like this, that are from home. And some of them are often in places like Maine, or way northern California, there's a guy there. There's a guy in Utah. There are some people that are kind of scattered out. And they get their jobs done pretty well. So it can be done, but I think it's easier being near a building. Which is why I haven't tried to move away from Madison, because it's very convenient that I can walk into the office quickly and deal with something, and then go back to my desk that's a five-minute drive away.

## Ageism and Experience

Matt: Do you think there's ageism in the gaming industry? Because I know that there's a little bit of that in the tech industry. Does that exist in the gaming world?

Mark: Oh yeah. Yeah. There's the joke that we're looking to hire somebody age 20 to 25 with 20 years experience and no family. So yeah, ageism is a problem. Again, it's hard to have a family and live in places like this [San Francisco] where the cost of living is high. A lot of the game companies know that. Also, more experienced developers that are older tend to be more expensive, because they've been working longer, they expect a bigger salary, if they have families they need to take care of them. So yeah, there's a certain degree of that that goes on, and a lot of it, in my opinion, is kind of short–sighted. As a developer it's kind of easy to look at it and say well, I could hire this one guy for X amount, or I could hire these two students for Y and Y and it's a lot cheaper. But, what people who look at it that way are missing out on is the fact that the experienced developer is not only gonna get the work done faster, their work is gonna be more resilient.

And what I mean by that, is, when you're programming, you can build a system that does something. But if you want to build it to do something in such a way that it's not gonna break under stressful conditions when there's too much going on in the game or whatever, there's a certain amount of experience that goes into building systems that are resilient to stress, frame rate, and number of guys running around on the screen, whatever.

There's a coder I work with named Steve; he's an awesome guy, who's been making games professionally since I was four years old. That guy can solve a problem instantly. And I'm sure he's more expensive than a college student that just started at our office. You know, when you give him a problem, he fixes it, and it's done, and you don't have to revisit it. And that's it.

So there's a tremendous value in having these more experienced employees. I do think a lot of game companies overlook that, but if they focus on the number of butts in seats and how cheaply they can get them, they miss out on what experience brings to the table.

Matt: Do you think it's important for the people that they hire in audio, is it critical that they play games themselves?

Mark: Definitely. You don't have to be a hardcore gamer in the sense you have to be playing games constantly, but I do think there's a lot of value in having somebody who plays other games, who knows what the market is like. We learn a lot by dissecting other people's games. Every time a new *Battlefront* game comes out, or a new *Battlefield* game comes out, we dissect it and we learn everything we can. And you get ideas that you bring to your own work. So there's definitely value in that sense. The other sense is, we're developing games. Everybody that we interact with in the other departments, including the design department, the art department, the animation department, they all play games. So, there's a certain language that develops from that, where people will say hey, we want to do this thing, and it's just like this scene in *Half-Life*, where such-and-such happened.

Which is kind of like the game development equivalent of "Hey, give me the snare drum used on that Zeppelin record," or something. You know what I mean? So you need to have that frame of reference, where when people start referring to other games, and talking about what was done on other stuff, you know what it is, or you can quickly go check it out and at least know what they're talking about. I do know some sound people that succeed despite not being super into games, but I think it's helpful. It's very helpful, yeah.

Matt: And back just to the discussion of ageism, if I go to a big box hardware store, like a Lowes or a Home Depot, if I have a problem that I can't figure out, I always seek out the oldest person there.

Mark: Absolutely.

Matt: Because I know they're gonna know. And I know that I'm not gonna get a distracted employee who's not focused on the problem and who causes me to have to go back two or three times just to solve the problem.

Mark: I agree completely.

Matt: So I see that value in older individuals working in any industry.

Mark: Absolutely.

Matt: Because I think, in the gaming industry, if you have older individuals, they have a sense of history. They have a sense of what's not worked in the past, the challenges of the past, and it puts everything into perspective. Would you agree with that?

Mark: Yeah, I totally agree with that. And again, that's why I feel like a lot of game companies are short sighted for not acknowledging that, and I feel like the work–life balance thing is a huge problem for us. It's been maybe four years since I saw numbers on it, but we have an organization called the International Game Developers Association that tracks stats about worker happiness in our industry. And I think it was roughly four years ago I last looked at the numbers, but the average turn rate for our industry was 10 years. So on average, people get sick of it and leave the game industry after 10 years. Because of quality–of–life issues.

And that's something we need to fix, if we want to keep those more experienced developers around. And in my 12 or 13 years of doing this, I gotta tell ya, the older developers tend to be the better ones. Just because they're more experienced. And it's the same thing, if I have a problem that I need some coder to help me with, or some animator to help me with, I kind of do the same thing you do at Lowes. I'm gonna go to the guy who knows what the hell they're doing because they've been doing it longer than I've been alive.

Matt: And the other advantage too is that older workers generally either have grown kids, or at the worst, their kids are in college or at the end of their college careers, and they're adults. And so their focus is really just to keep money coming in for their older years. It's an interesting thing, you know, because age plays a huge role in a lot of different industries, and it's dealt with in different ways in different industries. And speaking of age, let's talk about retirement for a second.

Mark: Sure.

## Money, Retirement, and Debt

Matt: Are you saving for retirement?

Mark: Absolutely, yes.

Matt: And is that based on a company 401K, or your own actions?

Mark: My own actions. I actually probably should sign up for my company's 401K, but I haven't done that. But we, my wife and I, have set up an automated cash flow payment system in savings, so everything is fully automated. My check deposits into an account, a portion of that gets transferred into another account that we can actually spend, a portion of that gets transferred into a retirement fund, a portion of that auto-pays all of our bills. It's kind of nice. I don't even think about bills, generally; it just kind of automatically happens. I read this great book years ago called *I Will Teach You to Be Rich*, by Ramit Sethi. He describes this idea of automating your money management so that you don't have to think about it, and by taking yourself out of the equation, you kind of automatically start saving and investing and stuff. And you don't screw it up by looking at it.

Matt: OK, I'll put that in the show notes on the Working Class Audio website for those who want to check that book out.

Mark: And, I've heard other people on your show say this, I do have a certain investment strategy with gear in terms of I try to buy higher quality stuff, and I try to buy it at the best prices possible, or used, and if we ever hit extremely hard times, I'll start liquidating my mic locker and things like that, which I'm sure will help. But yes, we absolutely are saving for retirement, and I don't want to leave my family hanging on that. And can I quickly say on finance: Don't go into debt for gear. Please, if you're listening or reading, don't go into debt for gear.

Matt: Yeah.

Mark: I just want to beat that into the heads of every student I ever talk to. Don't go into debt for gear. That's such a huge deal.

Matt: Are you speaking from experience?

Mark: Oh, yeah. Yeah. Well, when I first got started, I took on a little bit of debt. I am debt free now. I will not buy anything unless I have cash to pay for it. It's an evil trap. Don't go into debt for gear. Ever. If you can't afford it.

Matt: God, it certainly is, man. That's my main mission right now, is to finish up the debt, and be done with it. I'm almost there.

Mark: Yes. You will be so happy when you get there, and I will congratulate you when it happens.

Matt: I think I'm gonna throw a party and put it all on a credit card!

Mark: It's wonderful feeling. It's a wonderful feeling to get out from under that rock, man. It's huge. It happened a couple years ago for us, and it's awesome.

Matt: And we talked about that, about mental health, how economic challenges can really affect mental health. I think when you're challenged in those areas, it affects your decision making, whereas if you're debt free, you have a happy home life, whatever that home life is, however it's structured. As long as it's happy, you can make smarter decisions about your audio world and your business without as much duress as you would if you're challenged in those areas.

Mark: Absolutely. And another thing I really believe in that's related to that, I believe in the idea of having debt to myself. So everything I've purchased, I've tracked, and I keep track of how much money my system has made me, so I'm kind of trying to pay myself off in a way, which I know sounds weird.

Matt: Wow. That is a level of detail I'd have to really focus on.

Mark: I think it comes from, again, working in games and having to plot everything out in Excel. I've got spreadsheets of every single thing I've ever purchased, down to every cable in my studio, documented with the price and everything. And I'm tracking whether I've paid all this stuff off to myself, even though I didn't take on debt to buy it. I'm kind of keeping track of how much money it's made me. I'd like to break even, so that I can get into the black in that sense, so I can say that my gear made me more money than I spent on it.

## Networking and Friendship

Matt: Do you proactively network with other people?

Mark: Definitely. Networking is a huge, huge deal in games. Just about every job I've ever gotten has been through knowing somebody. So I network a lot, and networking is, it's a weird thing. I'm not the greatest at social interaction, my wife is the social butterfly, I tend to be the quiet one. Even though I'm just babbling endlessly here.

Matt: You're in your element, here.

Mark: Yeah, yeah. Well, we're talking audio stuff. But, my big thing on networking is, don't network to get work, network to make friends. And the reason I say that is because audio people tend to be some of the nicest people in the world. I've got my best friend in the world now, a guy I'd call if I ever killed somebody—I'm not gonna kill somebody! But if I had to hide a body, I would call him. He's an audio guy, and he's a guy I met a little over 10 years ago. And I've made some of my best friends in life through audio, and if you network to get work, people can sense that, and they know you're interacting with them because you're hoping to get something out of them.

If you network to make friends, that's when real connections happen, and work eventually comes anyway. So I usually tell people, network to make friends; don't network just to get work. And the other big thing is, find ways to give back to the community. And if you want to be selfish about it, you can say well, if you give back to the community, eventually people will start giving back to you. But if you just give back to people and be kind, (A) it feels great, it's a nice thing to do. And I do what I can on that front, and a lot of us in game audio do. We share things that we learn, or we show off tools, we teach people things that we have learned or things we're doing or whatever.

But (B) it's just a good way, if you can provide some value to the community, that kind of builds a sense of worth in you among other people, and that'll help in that effort as well. Networking is huge, but I think taking a generosity kind of approach to it is the best way to go. Give without expecting anything back, and you will probably get back in the end anyway. That's just generally how it works. At least it's been my experience in game audio, I don't know if it's the same in music, but you tell me.

Matt: I guess it depends on the personality.

Mark: OK.

Matt: But I love what you're saying about networking to be friends. I think Mike Wells (WCA #113), in his interview, talked about a very similar approach. If people want you and appreciate your talents, they know how to find you.

Mark: Yeah.

Matt: And if they have a good sense of you as a person, they're more likely to want to hire you.

Mark: I agree completely.

Matt: Because they know that they can reach out and you're trustworthy, and you're a good hang, and one of them.

Mark: Absolutely.

Matt: Well Mark, this has been great to talk to you here in this Starbucks with Celine Dion playing behind us.

Mark: Yeah, it's a little awkward.

Matt: Yeah. Well, thank you for meeting me.

Mark: Thank you, and quickly, I'm sorry to gush here, but thank you for doing this podcast. When I first communicated with you in late 2015 when my kids were just born—they were born premature, they were in NICU for a couple of months—I was staying near the hospital with them, and I listened. I had just discovered Working Class Audio around that time, and I listened to almost every podcast you had recorded up to that point. And it gave me something to focus on and do while I was dealing with that, so thank you for doing this podcast.

Matt: Oh, man. It's my pleasure.

Mark: It was a huge sanity saver while I was stuck there, waiting for my kids to get out of the hospital. So thank you.

Matt: Wow. Well, thank you. That's quite the compliment.

Mark: Thank you.

# Guests of the Working Class Audio Podcast

Over the past four years, I've had the pleasure to interview an incredible line-up of guests on the WCA Podcast, including the following:

Vance Powell, Tchad Blake, Frank Socorro, Streaky, Doug Clarke, Mixerman, Christopher Scott Cooper, Pete Lyman, Fela Davis, Pete Weiss, Adam Rossi, Sherry Klein, Karrie Keyes, Brian Gibbs, Sara Carter, Drew Vandenberg, Ryan Earnhardt, Will Sadler, David Cook, Lee Bothwick, Justin Weis, Kendal Osborne, Aaron Youngberg, Joshua Brooks, Joe Tessone, Craig Bowen, Mike Kennerty, Gary Noble, Bobby Owsinski, Daniel Holter, Brad Phillips, Zack Ohren, Phil Greiss, Adam Muñoz, Jack Endino, Jonathan Wyner, Mark Needham, Lucy J Mitchell, Kevin Army, James Ivey, Billy Decker, Ken Sluiter, Dave Collins, Steve Albini, John Karr, Matt Donner, Joe Costable, Matt Allison, Eddie Kramer, Dana Jae, Justin Perkins, Andrew Maury, James Tuttle, Katie Tavini, David Glasser, Jim Homes, Dom Morley, Bill Smith, Rene Coronado, Jack Shirley, Rocky Gallo, Tim Randolph, Chris Selim, Robert Scovill, Ryan Massey, Anthony Gravino, Kevin Becka, Jacquire King, Andrew Oswald, Alan Evans, Ian Shepherd, Ronan Chris Murphy, Andy Reed, Brad Smalling, Frank Pappalardo, Craig Schumacher, My Mix with the Masters brothers (Noam Levinberg, Rishi Bradoo, Eduardo Molina Goigoux, Jeremy Glover, Chris Brandes, Brett Bullion, Peo Hedin, Horacio Bolz, Ryan Worsley, Matthias Ortner, Guillaume Charret, Manuel Egger, Vincent Bonanno, Oded Davidov, Bas Kennis and Gilles Olivesi ) Peterson Goodwyn, Michael James, Owen Curtin, Jon O'Brien, Kurt Andress, Jim Greer, Will Russell, Tucker

Martine, Tyler Crowder, Cesar Mejia, Kurt Ballou Monte Vallier, Mike Wells, Frank Wolf, Nathan Harlow, Ben Lindell, Andy Freeman, Justin Pizzoferrato, Chris Montgomery, Chris Graham, Don Zientara, Michael Ashby, Andy Deguara, Pat Patten, Frank McDonough, Leff Lefferts, Stephen Hart , Cookie Marenco, Rob Schnapf, Stewart Cararas, Matt Ross-Spang, J.J. Blair, Brad Wood, Scott Wiley, David Barbe, Chuck Zwicky, Camden Stoddard, Lij Shaw, Ben Hirschfield , Scott Goodrich, Willie Samuels, Lolly Lewis, Emmit Brooks, Jeremy Goody, Brian Hood, Pablo Munguia, Justin Phelps, Drew Bollman, Jessica Thompson, Dave Fridmann, Chris Dugan, Andrew Stern, Gary Hobish, Mitch Dane, Tremaine Williams, John Schimpf, Mike Kalajian, Niko Bolas, Al Schmitt, Steve Genewick, Magnus Lindberg, John Paterno, Matt Wright, Graham Hick, Brad Brooks, Johnny Sangster, Joey Sturgis, Maor Appelbaum, TW Walsh, Brian McTear, Tardon Feathered, Jim Scott, The Pellicci Brothers, Josh Roberts, Ben Bernstein, Sebastien Richard, Darrell Thorp, Robert Preston, Peter Doell, Larry Crane, F. Reid Shippen, Bill Simpkins, John Vanderslice, Matt Wallace, Piper Payne, Eli Crews, Eric Valentine, Greg Wurth, Nino Moschella, John Greenham, Daniel Cantor, Sean McLaughlin, Warren Huart, Catherine Vericolli, Mark Rubel, Joe Barresi, Myles Boisen, Allen Farmelo, Bruce Kaphan, Michael Beinhorn, John Congleton, Dan Jaspar, John Siket, Tim Palmer, Gary Phillips, Ryan Hewitt, Michael Rosen, Doug Kallmeyer, Don Gunn, Matt Kelley, David v.R. Bowles, Ross Hogarth, Jonah Strauss, Jeff Powell, Sylvia Massy, Billy Anderson, Michael Starita, Gabriel Shepard, Scott Evans, Steve Silverstein, Robert L. Smith, John Cuniberti, David Wheeler, Hillary Johnson, Laura Dean, Peter B. Clarke, Cliff Truesdell, Chuck Smith, Cole WIlliams, Andrew Stess, Sammy Rothman, Charlene Gibbs, Loic Maestracci, David Bryce, Jerry Stucker, Buddy Saleman, Michael Romanowski, Paul Stubblebine, Bob Hodas, Larry Hirsch, Gil Norton, Joe Chiccarelli, Michael Molenda, Neal Brietbarth, Soundgirls.org, Björgvin Benediktsson, Kerry Rose

Thanks to all of you!

# About Matt Boudreau

Matt Boudreau is an audio engineer as well as the creator and host of the critically acclaimed podcast *Working Class Audio*. As a drummer, Matt's early career took him through the maze of the music industry while he toured and recorded with a series of bands, winning and losing record deals and learning how records were made on a large scale. From his early exposure to making records with Joe Chiccarelli, Gil Norton, and Larry Hirsch, Matt traded drumsticks for faders in 1994 when his passion for audio took over and became his focus. Since then Matt has been through the ups and downs of studio ownership and freelance recording, which ultimately lead to the creation of the Working Class Audio podcast.

Matt currently lives in the Bay Area with his wife and kids, working out of his home studio mixing and mastering as well as recording bands at his favorite Bay Area studios including Sharkbite, 25th Street Recording, and New Improved Recording.